scale up faster

scale up faster

The Secrets of the World's Quickest-Growing Bootstrapped Companies

PETE MARTIN

AN INC.
ORIGINAL

An Inc. Original
New York, New York
www.anincoriginal.com

Distributed by Greenleaf Book Group

For ordering information or special discounts for bulk purchases, please contact Greenleaf Book Group at PO Box 91869, Austin, TX 78709, 512.891.6100.

Design and composition by Greenleaf Book Group
Cover design by Greenleaf Book Group and Aaniyah Ahmed
Cover images used under license from ©Adobestock.com/jolygon

Publisher's Cataloging-in-Publication data is available.

Print ISBN: 978-1-63909-048-8

eBook ISBN: 978-1-63909-049-5

To offset the number of trees consumed in the printing of our books, Greenleaf donates a portion of the proceeds from each printing to the Arbor Day Foundation. Greenleaf Book Group has replaced over 50,000 trees since 2007.

Printed in the United States of America on acid-free paper

25 26 27 28 29 30 31 32 10 9 8 7 6 5 4 3 2 1

First Edition

This book is dedicated to all you entrepreneurs, founders, and business leaders trying to grow your companies, change your small part of the world, and make an impact—and doing so by bootstrapping your growth.

You are the heroes, not the unicorn founders.
You deserve the spotlight—step into it.

bootscaling

(BOOT • skayl • ing) *noun*

a trademarked method for growing much faster than your competitors without selling your company (and your soul) to outside investors to do so

Antonym: blitzscaling: achieving massive scale and growth by raising buckets of cash to get there

CONTENTS

PART III: CAPITAL

PART IV: STRATEGIC EXECUTION

PART V: LEADERSHIP

FOREWORD

Scale Up Faster deserves a prominent place on your bookshelf. It dives deep into the DNA of the 1 percent of the fastest-growing companies within the prestigious *Inc.* 5000. These are the bootstrapped scale-ups, unburdened by the constraints of venture capital, who defy the odds and scale faster than their competitors.

Pete Martin, a kindred spirit in the growth movement, has embarked on a two-and-a-half-year odyssey to unlock the secrets of this top 1 percent. *Scale Up Faster* is not a compilation of generic business advice. It's a treasure trove of battle-tested strategies for entrepreneurs who yearn to break free from the pack.

The stories within these pages are not just narratives of success; they are blueprints for anyone who dares to dream big enough to pursue those dreams with unwavering tenacity.

This book unveils the secrets these bootstrapped fast-growth companies employ to:

- Attract and retain A-players who are as hungry for growth as they are
- Forge a rock-solid culture that fuels innovation and execution

- Master the art of strategic planning and ruthlessly prioritize for maximum impact
- Develop a laser-sharp customer focus and dominate their niche

And a whole lot more. As you turn the pages, prepare to challenge your assumptions, reimagine your strategies, and implement the growth hacks that will propel your business to unprecedented heights.

Remember, growth is a choice. *Scale Up Faster* equips you with the knowledge and inspiration to make that choice, break the chains of mediocrity, and join the ranks of the extraordinary.

It is my pleasure to write this foreword, as this book speaks to the core of what it means to build a regenerative, scalable business.

To the ambitious entrepreneurs and business leaders reading this book: You are the catalysts for change and the architects of the future. May the insights in the book inspire you to scale new peaks and realize your full potential.

Scale up faster, not just in business, but in impact, legacy, and the indelible mark you leave on the world.

VERNE HARNISH
Founder of Entrepreneurs' Organization
and author of *Scaling Up*

PREAMBLE

They've never run a business before. They have no business plan. They think cold calling is the right way to grow. They're not exactly sure what business they're in. They're a little bit angry, and they have chips on their shoulders. They disdain how everyone else does things and are a bit messy organizationally. They don't have college degrees from top universities and they are still pretty young—in their late thirties. But they're driven, tenacious, authentic, thoughtful, motivated, determined, resourceful, confident (maybe even cocky), and innovative.

Based on this profile, would you invest in these CEOs and their companies?

It turns out, even if you wanted to, you couldn't because these founders and CEOs didn't ask for external capital—primarily because they didn't know or think they could (although one CEO tried and got turned down more than one hundred times—and has the spreadsheet to prove it!).

It's too bad you couldn't invest because it turns out that they all were, and are, amazing bootstrapped fast-growth companies—what I call BFGs.

In this book, I explore how these companies and their extraordinarily ordinary founders grew so fast with nothing but grit, tenacity, resourcefulness, and a little luck.

If you are looking for the magical silver bullet, the secret of business growth that's never been revealed until right now, that little switch you can press or the lever you can pull that will automagically unleash containers full of cash and new business, well then, you're going to be disappointed. Go ahead and return the book.

But if you are looking for timeless, industry-agnostic, field-tested, practical, and actionable advice on the strategic frameworks, strategies, and tactics used by America's fastest-growing companies, then buckle up, settle down, and get out a highlighter or notebook (virtually, if you're reading this online), because this book is for you.

As the authors from McKinsey and Company who wrote *CEO Excellence: The Six Mindsets That Distinguish the Best Leaders from the Rest* so eloquently put it, "We're not just going to have an instruction manual that says, 'Here's how to play guitar.' We're going to say, 'Here's how you become Eddie van Halen or Eric Clapton, as opposed to a weekend guitarist.'"[1]

And since I'm a drummer, I'll change it slightly to say this is not a manual on how to play the drums; it's how you become Neil Peart or Pete Martin. (See what I did there? If you don't know who either of those drummers are, google them—or at least google Neil.)

Like the McKinsey book, I give you the tools to have an exceptional company and be an exceptional CEO. Like most things, you can be exceptional if you model yourself after (rather than copy) exceptional people.

But here's the truth. The founders and CEOs in this book are not exceptional. They are ordinary people doing extraordinary things with their companies. I want to emphasize this because anyone leading a small or medium-sized company can take the same steps and, with a bit of luck (I talk about that later) can achieve similar results.

Sadly, the business media focuses on both unicorn founders and charismatic CEOs. Why? Because they're cool, fun to interview, and fun for us to read about. The good news is that many of the best (some might say boring) founder CEOs are hiding in plain sight and growing amazing companies—in many cases, much faster than practically everyone else.

I shine the spotlight on these unique individuals and their companies because that's who we should be modeling ourselves after and learning from, not the celebrity CEOs we all read about. And especially not the myriad unicorn founders who've been trusted with hundreds of millions, or even billions, of investor capital only to squander it as so many have done in the past few years.

I want to share the secrets of these exceptional CEOs and their leadership teams to help you grow your business faster than ever before without having to give up control (equity, personal guarantees, etc.) to venture capitalists (VCs), private equity (PE) firms, banks, or anyone who is going to keep you up at night.

I hope to be your guide in making your growth and scaling journey easier.

ACKNOWLEDGMENTS

I owe this book to all the extraordinary, humble, and selfless business leaders who were so generous with their time, patient with my never-ending questions, and open with their personal and professional experiences: Aasha Anam, Scott Andrew, Kelly Bolton, Robert Brill, Russell Brunson, Michael Chavira, Carlos Chilin, Darren Conrad, Megan Crutcher, Kurt Donnell, Jules Dykes, Simon Elsbury, Daniel Evans, Christina Fiasconaro, Bobby Frazitta, David Freedman, Lauren Goveo, Brandon Green, Et Halstead, Keith Higginbotham, Mark Hodges, Ruston Hughes, Ellen Hughes, Robbyn Jackson, Zarrar Kahn, Stan Konar, Naveen Krishnamurthy, Alex Love, Gina Lujan, Kyle Mitnick, Neelu Modali, Jonathan Moisan, Linda Monsour, Sufian Munir, John Newton, Chloe Oddleifson, Zack Onisko, Neil Patel, Bob Peterson, Son Pham, KorbyQuan Reed, Justin Ring, Jess Rodriguez, Christy Rosensteel, Frankie Russo, Michael Sacca, Claudia Schiepers, Lawrence Scotland, Christina Stembel, Kat Taylor Simonyi, Kate Turner, Don Wenner, Lindsey Whalen Draska, Jerry Williams, Jim Wilson, Kevin Wong, Jamie Woods, and Brion Yarnell. They are the models of business success, and I hope their stories inspire other equally capable founders, entrepreneurs, and business leaders to bootscale their companies like these leaders have. I'm forever grateful to all of them. To show our collective appreciation for these companies, be sure to check out and purchase their products and services that I reference in the book!

For their support and help with layout, editing, production, and launch, I thank the outstanding Greenleaf/*Inc.* team, including Jen Glynn, Valerie Howard, Rachael High, Dee Kerr, Rebecca Logan, Heather Stettler, Cameron Stein, and Aaron Teel.

Many thanks go to my beta readers, who helped make sure the book was useful and beneficial for other entrepreneurs and business leaders: John Dyer, Kimberly Dyer, Brian Kalakay, Anthony Milia, Chris Perez, and Andrea Ruosi.

Thanks go to those who pushed me to finish the book and get it launched properly: Heidi Baldwin, Debbie Hoffman, Megan O'Malley, Ashley de Tello, Alexis Snell, Cierra Warner, and Amber Vilhauer.

And my thanks go to my amazing family—Torie, Ellie, Laine, and Julie—for their undying support and endless encouragement!

INTRODUCTION

My Book's Origin Story

I conceived this project around eight years ago after I sold my last business, a consulting firm, to KPMG. Selling that company in 2014 was my fourth exit, and I felt pretty accomplished. So, of course, like every person who wants to share their success with the world, I began scripting out my success story, meaning I started to write a book—in fact, the precursor to this one.

And, of course, I knew I'd sell millions of books!

I'm not sure when it hit me, but at some point along the way, I knew in my heart that no one other than my family and a few friends gave a damn about my story. That realization smacked me in the face (it's really tough being tough on yourself). I realized that in the greater context of business, I was nothingsville.

I've always been a huge fan of Jim Collins's seminal book, *Good to Great*, and the rest of his books. But because the stories and evidence in his most successful books are based on large public companies, I wanted to do the same for smaller, fast-growing private companies.

I resolved to write a book similar to Jim's (that's a pretty bold statement, I know!) for the millions of founders, CEOs, and entrepreneurs of smaller private companies who want to grow faster and still retain control of their businesses and their senses. I ate a huge slice of humble pie and started my research. And I'm so glad I did.

I've learned so much over the past two and a half years, studying the best of the best and going deep with really generous business leaders who gave their time to help me understand how they accomplished their amazing growth. I'm honored and grateful to share some nuggets of wisdom with you, my fellow crazy entrepreneur, so that you achieve much greater success than I ever have—on par with the people and companies covered in this book.

Society and the business media put a bright spotlight on unicorn companies and their founders, but lost in the shadows are the millions of founders scratching it out every day to earn a living and create something bigger than themselves. They should be celebrated too, and that's what this book is all about!

Sigmund Freud purportedly once said, "The years of struggle will strike you as the most beautiful." To be clear, the stories in this book aren't all rainbows and unicorns. Every one of the CEOs I interviewed has experienced serious setbacks in their business, but they all persisted through the tough times to continue their growth. We cover these stories to let you know that their journeys of exceptional growth were filled with potholes large enough to swallow whole cars.

Growing a company faster than your industry average without accepting external capital from VCs, PE firms, investment bankers, and others is really hard—and really worth it. As Kyle Mitnick, the founder and former CEO of Advertise Purple said, "External capital is a crutch and doesn't allow you to really know if the business is viable and scalable."[1]

Enjoy your journey. *You can do this!*

Why Focus on Growing Faster?

Without continual growth and progress, such words as *improvement*, *achievement*, and *success* have no meaning.
—ATTRIBUTED TO BENJAMIN FRANKLIN

As Robert Plant from Led Zeppelin famously wrote, there are two paths you can take. Every business owner and CEO gets to make their own choice to (a) grow faster each year or (b) take their foot off the gas and let their company coast. Coasting is fine for many business owners, but greater personal wealth and long-term personal freedom generally come from generating size and scale. In addition, your ability to have a positive impact on the communities and stakeholders you care about improves with size and scale.

I don't subscribe to the classic line "grow or die," but I do believe that if you don't continue to grow, the risk of becoming irrelevant increases. Top-performing employees won't stick around a company that isn't growing, customers will eventually find other suppliers if you're not innovating and improving, and the personal worth you have wrapped up in your business will begin to diminish.

I believe growing and scaling faster, when you control your destiny by bootstrapping, provides substantial long-term benefits. These long-term benefits have a positive impact on the quality of your team and increase your profits, your enterprise value, and ultimately your personal and financial freedom.

I came across a recent article that further substantiates the key insights in this book. Research done by start-up lender Capchase found that raising venture capital did not result in significantly higher growth rates compared to bootstrapped companies over a one-year period. The report analyzed financial data from nine hundred early-stage SaaS companies that had between $1 and $15 million in annual recurring revenue. The data set was split almost evenly between bootstrapped and venture-backed companies. The report found that between June 2022 and the end of May 2023, venture-backed companies experienced an average 42.8 percent year-over-year growth rate. Bootstrapped companies had an average year-over-year growth rate of 44 percent.[2]

Better yet, the report found that bootstrapped companies achieved similar growth levels with significantly lower customer acquisition costs compared to venture-backed counterparts. This cost-conscious approach allowed bootstrapped start-ups to maintain a higher customer lifetime value to customer acquisition cost ratio (LTV/CAC), indicating more efficient resource allocation. The bootstrapped companies had ratios around eight to one versus less than two to one for VC-backed firms, indicating substantially more efficient spending.[3]

The founders of these bootstrapped companies emphasized the importance of being financially prudent and focusing on ROI, suggesting that they could execute growth strategies effectively without additional capital. (This is exactly what the BFGs did, and I am trying to help you do the same thing!)

I've had the fortune of working with and advising hundreds of business leaders and entrepreneurs, and I've never met one who didn't want their company to grow faster than it had the previous year. I believe humans have an innate growth gene, and since companies are simply a collection of people, it's natural for faster growth to be a central focus of most businesses.

The Rule of 40 is a metric used, particularly in the technology sectors, to evaluate the delicate balance between growth and profitability. The Rule of 40 states that the annual growth rate plus the net profit margin should equal or exceed 40 percent. For instance, if a company grows 25 percent per year with a net margin of 15 percent, it meets the Rule of 40.

This threshold doesn't apply to all companies or industries, especially where industry margins are substantially lower (here's looking at you, retail). Still, it's an excellent way to balance the competing demands of investing in growth or enhancing profitability. The thinking goes that rapid growth often requires significant investment and may come at the expense of short-term profitability. Conversely, focusing too much on profitability can stifle growth, so by using this rule, proper growth can be maintained. Keeping both in balance is what our BFGs excelled at (even though very few knew of the Rule of 40). Companies that adhere to the Rule of 40 tend to have higher valuations than their peers because they demonstrate the ability to grow while also being mindful of profitability, which is a sign of efficient management and operational effectiveness.

When I asked John Warrillow, author of *Built to Sell* and founder of the Value Builder System, if he would evaluate and endorse my book, he hesitated. (Ah, c'mon John, give a guy a break!) He was worried that the key message of this book was to grow at all costs, to the detriment of focusing on the company's overall value. Thankfully, that's not the key message. (To be transparent, we leverage the Value Builder System at our firm, so John and I are fully aligned on our passion for increasing the personal wealth of business owners.)

The good news is that balancing faster growth and scale with profitability is one of the biggest levers for increasing business valuation. In simple terms, faster growth (at good profit margins) equals a more valuable company.

Eponymous VC firm Andreessen Horowitz recently discovered that the most highly valued companies excelled at growth vis-à-vis (don't you love that word?!) their competitors (just like our beloved BFGs). They analyzed the valuations of the top fifty companies founded after 2000 by market cap. They compared their valuations as a function of free cash flow margin versus a function of annual growth rates. They found that growth trumped margins for becoming a more valuable company.[4]

The reason for this is quite elementary (that is, the math is elementary). If your company grows at 30 percent over the next five years instead of 20 percent, it will become 1.5 times bigger. If margins remain constant, you'll receive a 50 percent higher multiple in today's terms, resulting in a company that is twice as valuable.

To assuage my friend John Warrillow, the bottom line is that focusing on growth does play a significant role (though it is not the only factor) in increasing your company's value and, in turn, your equity wealth as an owner.

The downside of growing faster—if you don't manage it properly—is that the risks get equally bigger. With faster growth and scale, the impact of every decision is magnified. As Scott Andrew, the founder, chairman of the board, CEO, and president of Retail Service Systems (RSS) noted, "That's one of the challenges of fast growth. It covers up a lot of bad decision making. You don't see it when you do start to slow down; then, all of a sudden, you see challenges you didn't notice before."[5]

Furthermore, if you don't learn how to delegate effectively, then pursuing faster growth can result in burnout (see Chapter 5) but overall, faster growth and larger scale are net positives. Not one of the CEOs in our BFG companies regretted pursuing faster growth and scale. This wasn't an ego thing to them; it was about having a bigger impact on more customers, team members, and the communities they serve.

So, assuming you believe faster growth and scale are good things (I suspect you do, since you're reading this book), let me tell you how I picked the companies to study for this book.

How I Conducted the Research

Feel free to skip this section if you trust me and don't care how I conducted my research.

I wanted to study the best of the best bootstrapped/self-funded companies that have consistently grown faster than their competitors. I call each of these a BFG—bootstrapped fast-growth company (clever, right?!).

I started with the list of companies in the *Inc.* 5000[6] from 2015–2022, which is a selection of self-nominated companies published by

Inc. magazine that ranks the fastest-growing privately held businesses in the United States. I consolidated the annual lists from all seven years then filtered the list to identify the companies that, on average, doubled their revenues for at least four consecutive years during that period. Growing at a rate of 100 percent every year for at least four years while self-funding/bootstrapping that growth is truly phenomenal, and I knew I would find nuggets of wisdom in the lessons learned from these companies.

Using this filter took approximately thirty thousand unique companies in my consolidated database down to 386. I then used public sources of capital funding such as CB Insights, Pitchbook, and others to eliminate the companies that I believed achieved their extraordinary growth because they raised gobs of capital. (As I like to say, give me $100 million in capital and, of course, I can grow faster too!)

Removing those externally funded companies whittled down the list to 324 companies to study. Coincidentally, the final list of 324 represents the top 1 percent of all *Inc.* 5000 companies over that seven-year period.

Then the real work began.

My team and I initially analyzed each one of those companies to identify any common themes. We looked at their websites, read articles about them, and reviewed the *Inc.* 5000 available data. As a result, we identified fifty-five companies that represented a cross section of the 324 companies. This group covered every industry, including business to consumer (B2C), business to business (B2B), business to government (B2G), real estate development, financial services, franchising, and so on to study deeper through personal interviews.

I set up one-on-one video interviews with the founders/CEOs of this cross-section of companies, in which I spent at least two hours asking them detailed questions about their background, origin stories, growth levers, and other topics. I then asked to speak with their executive teams. The CEOs who allowed me access to their business leaders (a cross section of twenty-eight companies) gave me the opportunity to look at the full functional breadth of their businesses (this is where it got really fun!). With their permission, I conducted one-on-one video interviews with their heads of HR/people, marketing, sales, operations, and finance.

I used technology to transcribe each video interview. I used both HUMINT (human intelligence) and a generative artificial intelligence (AI) application (ChatGPT 4.0) on the transcripts from all the interviews to look for patterns in the answers to the questions.

My team and I then pulled content from the websites of all 324 companies to extract the words they use to describe their culture and the characteristics they use to select team members. We input those data into ChatGPT 4.0 to look for patterns in how they created these high-growth cultures and built their teams (you can find these results in Part I). I used the financial data provided for the *Inc.* 5000 lists along with more detailed financial information to calculate the cash conversion cycles for these companies to determine how they could grow so fast on internally generated cash flow. I detail this analysis in Part III.

In this book, I highlight eleven companies of the fifty-five I interviewed. These eleven companies are exceptional examples of the frameworks and strategies in this book, although the lessons from all 324 companies are represented here.

The quantitative and qualitative data from all this research forms the basis for this book. There are many quotes from our study participants throughout. Some of the quotes are exactly what the individual said, and some have been edited for grammar, clarity, or contextual reasons without changing the meaning. I am honored and excited to provide you the opportunity to learn directly from their voices and not just mine. I hate to admit it, but many of them are funnier than I am (those who know me know this is hard for me to admit), and all of them are class acts and exceptional businesspeople.

A Profile of the Companies and Leaders in This Book

Annual revenue for the 324 BFG companies we studied ranged from $8.0 million up to $2.0 billion with an average of $78.3 million and a median of $24.3 million.[7] The median year-over-year growth was 149.7 percent, and the average was 163.9 percent. The average number of employees was 260, and the median was 71. And finally, the average age of these companies was thirteen years—not a long time to achieve this type of success.

The entrepreneurs, founders, and CEOs who lead these BFGs don't fit neatly into any particular demographic or background. They are all ordinary individuals with an extraordinary ability to grow their companies consistently and should be considered incredibly successful from a business perspective. This is great news because that means *anyone* can achieve the same sort of success these people have. And it's important to note that anyone who attempts entrepreneurship, even if they fail, should be considered successful because they took the initiative to create something.

On average, these founders started their companies at age thirty-four, and they are now an average of forty-two years old. The average educational level was a bachelor's degree, and virtually none of their degrees were from the most prestigious colleges. Most had never started a company before their current one, although a few had start-ups in college or previous businesses that failed. (This means they learned what *not* to do!)

When I interviewed the CEOs, the words they used most frequently to describe themselves included *driven*, *authentic*, *thoughtful*, *useful*, *tenacious*, *motivated*, *determined*, *resourceful*, *confident*, and *innovative*. As one might expect, they all had a high tolerance for risk, and they felt in control of their environment because they knew that whatever life threw at them, they had control over their response to it.

Each one of the CEOs I interviewed successfully guided their businesses through COVID-19, and many of them grew faster because of the decisions they made during that time.

Virtually all of them are voracious readers and continuous learners.

One thing was a complete surprise to me. The book cited more than any other as a guide to their decisions was *Meditations* by Marcus Aurelius. (Who would have seen that coming?!)

A Little about Me

I've personally started, scaled, and sold four companies, and I have several more which are still active. When people ask me why I started so many companies, I tell them that I am a genetically encoded entrepreneur. My grandfather, father, and brother all had their own businesses, and my sisters had some side hustles, too.

I basically flunked out of my first semester of college and decided to start a car-leasing company at the age of eighteen. I was the classic snot-nosed kid who arrogantly thought he knew everything about business, and boy did the world slap me some new lessons. After grinding for a few years with minimal success, I sold the business for a loss and decided to try college again. I tested out of almost a year of college. (If you want to save a ton of money on college, check out the College Level Examination Program [CLEP] exams.) This time, I dove in seriously.

Even though I had my head down studying, I still wanted to keep my entrepreneurial skills sharp, so I started a local chapter of the Association of Collegiate Entrepreneurs (ACE). ACE was started by the OG of business growth, Verne Harnish—considered by many as the original "Growth Guy."

Verne is the founder of several world-renowned entrepreneurship organizations including the Young Entrepreneurs' Organization, ACE, and most importantly the founder and CEO of Gazelles, Inc.

(now called Scaling Up). As the founder and CEO of Scaling Up, a global executive education and coaching company with more than two hundred partners on six continents, Verne has spent the past four decades helping companies scale up. I give my deep gratitude to Verne and the legacy he has left in the world of growth and scaling organizations.

My participation in ACE provided me with a foundational framework for how to grow and scale my companies faster, and I've used that framework in every one of the companies I started, scaled, and eventually sold. I also made the lion's share of my mistakes running companies and have learned quite a few lessons (a.k.a. *failures*) along the way. But I don't regret or dwell on any of my mistakes or failures because the battle scars have made me a better leader. Similarly, every one of the CEOs I interviewed were honest and vulnerable about the mistakes they had made. I hope I can save you from a few additional battle wounds by sharing those lessons with you in this book.

How This Book Is Organized

The parts of this book riff off of Verne's 4 Decisions framework but with a Pete twist. Verne's 4 Decisions framework includes people, strategy, execution, and cash. I borrowed and revised these concepts, and the first four parts of the book ("Team," "Customers," "Capital," and "Strategic Execution") are based on those concepts. The fifth part of the book is on leadership. I arranged the parts in the order I consider to be most useful to business leaders trying to grow and scale faster.

I focus on your team in the first part because your team, whether they are employees, partners, or contractors, will almost always define your long-term success, which includes you as the CEO/founder.

There is no specific mention of customers in many of the business strategy books in the market today, but the ability to acquire, support, and expand the customer base is the primary success factor in all the BFGs I cover in the book. And, at an elemental level, without customers, there is no business.

Growth takes cash. Our BFGs have been exceptional at preserving cash, figuring out ways to make a dollar go farther, and being creative in getting past the obstacles of cash flow constraints. Cash flow issues are one of the biggest reasons why businesses fail, so figuring out how to improve cash flow as you grow is fundamental.

The fourth part focuses on strategic execution. All day-to-day decisions are not equal so deciding what to focus on and what not to focus on can make a profound difference in your success. Combining the right strategic decisions with solid execution is paramount. One without the other leads to either operational chaos or directionless efficiency that will most likely eventually slam you into a wall.

The final part is on leadership because your company will only grow as fast as you and your leaders. Our BFG leaders were relatively early in their professional careers when they started their companies, so they had a lot to learn to grow and scale quickly. Every founder and CEO I spoke with had a professional development process consisting of extensive reading, mastermind groups (most were informal as opposed to Vistage, Scaling Up, or similar organizations), and formal mentee relationships. They knew that creating a learning organization was fundamental to their success, so they enthusiastically supported companywide professional development programs.

The Biggest Takeaways from My Research

The following list summarizes some key highlights from the research. Each chapter illuminates these broad findings and tells the stories of these companies, but this quick list of findings will get your brain warmed up:

- Virtually none of the companies had a formal business plan.
- Most didn't seek external capital because they didn't think they would get it; the few that tried were unsuccessful.
- Each one of these companies is exceptionally lean at the leadership level—there are way more doers than leaders/managers in their companies.
- They all focused heavily on one primary method of generating revenue and growing sales.
- They all deployed strategies to ensure they could hold onto and grow their cash positions.
- Most created communities around their businesses as a low-cost and complementary way to attract new customers.
- They all had explicit culture-fit traits they were looking for when they hired their top-performing team members.
- They were all a bit messy—I expected to see super-efficient, well-oiled machines. What I found was that many were constant works-in-process.
- They grew faster when they started measuring the business for the key inputs that truly drove growth.
- They took a while to find the core of their business, but once they did, they stayed focused entirely on it and didn't stray from it.
- They didn't focus on what their competitors were doing—they focused on what made them unique, like the Guru button (more on this later).

I suppose you could stop reading now if you wanted to, but I think you'll learn a lot by reading on!

As a result of my research, we were able to get to the heart of these companies' successes, which led us to call into question many powerfully entrenched ideas about how to grow a company. Although I will detail some common business growth strategies, a decent number of ideas contradict the ideas extolled by many of today's gurus.

To wrap up my findings into a nice package or methodology, I tried, but failed, to come up with a super fancy, sexy acronym for growing and scaling up faster (SUF—I don't think so). Instead of an acronym, I decided to call this approach to scaling up faster bootscaling, which I define as growing much faster than your competitors without selling your company (and your soul) to outside investors. I think many business experts believe that you can't grow fast on internally generated cash flow and therefore raising external funds is necessary, but our BFGs proved otherwise.

To successfully bootscale, leaders need to strategically work on all four core areas of what I refer to as pillars of power (team, customers, capital, and strategic execution). These pillars create the foundation for faster growth, sustainable scale, optimal cash flow, and maximum business value, which are fundamental to the long-term success of any business. Each pillar (and part of this book) is organized into what I call virtuous functional capabilities (VFC) that represent the unique individual processes that companies must master over the long term to effectively scale up. These VFCs are specified at the beginning of each part to identify the discrete processes involved with each functional area. For instance, in Part I, "Team," you must attract candidates and then hire, retain, grow, and release them, so the VFC for the team pillar is attract → hire → support → grow → release. I recognize that each capability is not completely independent from other integrated processes, but I use them as a way to make each functional area easier to follow. (At least, I hope so!)

These VFCs (I know this all sounds very management consulting-ish!) within the pillars of power is the core of our Bootscaling Method, which has become a proven strategic framework to accelerate faster profitable growth by leveraging the same strategies, tactics, and tools used by the fastest-growing companies in this book.

One final important note.

The strategies, frameworks, philosophies, and actions we identified in my research correlate with the performance patterns we found. Still, I cannot claim a definitive causal relationship. Securing nonpublic data was tough enough, and running controlled trials would be virtually impossible, so I cannot claim cause and effect with 100 percent certainty. Nevertheless, I feel confident in the lessons covered in the book. Consequently, if you don't follow the advice in the book, it will be at the peril of growing slower than you'd like or giving up control to the banks, VCs, and PE firms who want to exploit the hidden power in your business before you do!

All of that aside, let's dig in to see what makes these companies so special.

> Building a successful business is more than just a path to financial independence; it's a deeply personal journey filled with emotional highs and lows. These aspects of entrepreneurship are as crucial as managing the business itself. To discover practical advice on how to manage your emotional journey of entrepreneurship, check out our Book Resources section at www.scaleupfaster.com/resources and download our ebook *The Monkey Mind: Navigating the Emotional Highs and Crushing Lows of Building a Successful Business.*

Meet Some of Our Star BFGs

To get started, I want to introduce you to a few of our BFGs to give you a sense of the diversity of the companies I studied, just in case you think these lessons don't apply to your business. (I know, you're unique.)

Although I studied 324 of the fastest-growing *Inc.* 5000 bootstrapped companies, I deeply analyzed, researched, and interviewed sixty-two leaders (CEOs and heads of sales, marketing, finance, people/team, and finance) to understand how they grew their sales faster than their competitors. I asked this select group of individuals more than 112 questions in more than eighty individual interviews to dig into their marketing, sales, and service functions to understand how they acquired, sold, and supported their customers. There are too many companies to list individually, so this summary of a few of them will give you some context for their industries and the ways they go to market. All of the companies described in the following pages are exceptional BFG case studies and are representative of their industry. I share additional insights about each of them in subsequent chapters.

JCW GROUP

Staffing and recruiting (B2B)
Primary customer acquisition channel: cold-calling and content development

JCW is a recruiting and staffing company headquartered in the UK with a significant presence in the United States and Europe. They have grown more than 1,500 percent from 2017 to 2022 and have been on the *Inc.* 5000 list five times in the past five years. They go to market primarily through cold-calling prospects supported by substantial industry-specific research from their marketing department.

Their number-one marketing lever is conducting research and publishing an up-to-date salary guide several times per year. The distribution of this key asset is tightly integrated with their sales teams, so when they are outbound calling on customers and prospects, they immediately deliver value. Daniel Evans, the former marketing director for JCW Group, explained it this way:

> We produce a Salary Guide every year, which provides updates on salaries, market trends, hiring bonuses, skills in demand, relocation, etc. Whatever the latest trends are, working from home, you name it. Even nine months after we publish the Guide, we get at least five thousand monthly downloads. People ask us when the next Guide will come out because the information is so valuable. But I think the biggest thing is that we make sure it's fully integrated with sales—it isn't just a marketing campaign. It's a sales and marketing campaign. The sales teams engage with it so well because it's valuable, and people request it. It's that sales engagement that makes it so successful.[8]

Their marketing approach is to provide as much value to prospective and existing customers as possible to create a platform of trust and authenticity. Their website is their number-one marketing tool (check it out—it's exceptional). They also work with their recruiters to develop their brand on LinkedIn, which helps broaden their reach and promote the company.

MINDPATH COLLEGE HEALTH (FORMERLY ACACIA COUNSELING AND WELLNESS)

Healthcare provider (B2C)
Primary customer acquisition channel: paid ads

Acacia Counseling and Wellness provides mental health and wellness services to college students in several markets in the western United States. Mindpath College Health acquired Acacia during the course of our research. Before they were acquired, Acacia grew 1092 percent from 2017 to 2022 and spent four years on the *Inc.* 5000 list. They learned quickly when rolling out new offices that each new location they expanded to had its own particular culture—California was very different from Minnesota and Texas even though they were all serving the same college student market. They eventually learned to test and warm up the market through relationship building and brand awareness with the community before launching and physically opening a new office. Acacia primarily relies on paid ads (mostly Google ads) to generate new patient traffic. As KorbyQuan Reed, brand manager for Mindpath College Health (formerly Acacia Counseling and Wellness) told me, "We did social media where we could, but mostly we focused on Google ads to help get people in the door. We complemented that with focused campaigns with University Services."[9]

RIVA SOLUTIONS

Government services provider (B2G)
Primary customer acquisition channel: direct field sales

RIVA Solutions is a federal government contracting firm headquartered in Reston, Virginia. RIVA stands for results, innovation, values, accountability. The company grew 452 percent during the research timeframe and spent four years consecutively on the *Inc.* 5000 list, which is extraordinarily difficult to do for a professional services firm focused on the public sector. RIVA is now a prime contractor supporting more than twenty federal agencies. They started by subcontracting to other firms that served as prime contractors until they grew out of the set-aside market for smaller companies. (A nice problem to have, right?) Once they grew out of the set-asides, they had to compete with the behemoth federal government contractors. Most similar firms can't make the leap, but RIVA has reinvented itself at each growth phase and continues to grow unabated.

Because of their market, they are selling into very large, complex, and by-the-book government procurement processes. Generating awareness of the company and its expertise and building long-term relationships are essential in their market, so they focus heavily on brand awareness through LinkedIn posts with thought leadership content focused on the topics their sales teams are bidding on. The goal is to have the company's subject matter experts create assets that the sales teams can use to get into the right places and events. Alex Stevens Love, vice president of marketing and communications for RIVA Solutions, explained it this way:

> I think the most important tactic for us has been digital [content] marketing. We have a pretty large community on LinkedIn, especially for a company our size, and we've built it organically. We haven't spent any money on advertising, pay-per-click ads, or anything like that, which means that our community is a lot more invested in the content. We get pretty high engagement in our posts, specifically on LinkedIn. We dabble in other channels, but LinkedIn is primarily where we get a lot of traction.[10]

DRIBBBLE

Marketplace for creative people (B2C)
Primary customer acquisition channel: SEO

Dribbble is a two-sided marketplace for creative people (graphic designers, etc.) to share their portfolios, find work, connect with like-minded people, and be hired by companies looking for creative talent. They grew 601 percent from 2017 to 2022 and have enjoyed their fifth listing in five years on the *Inc.* 5000 list. And they did all of this with a small, 100 percent remote team. Their growth mainly came from organic SEO, which became less cost-effective as their VC-backed competitors began spending gobs of money competing with them to pick up market share.

They are avid testers utilizing A/B and multivariate testing. They constantly measure their return on ad spend (ROAS) and CAC to ensure they are profitable in acquiring new customers. Lawrence Scotland, vice president of marketing for Creative Market, explained their approach to me:

> I think content marketing and SEO have gotten us to a certain place and have been real levers of growth in the past. . . . As we move forward, paid marketing and things like referral programs are our ways that will use the new levers that we're introducing to drive incremental growth.[11]

DLP CAPITAL

Real estate development firm
Primary customer acquisition channel: in-person events

With more than $5 billion of assets under management, DLP Capital has been on the *Inc.* 5000 for eleven consecutive years. DLP Capital is a high-growth impact investor that leverages real-estate-backed capital to build wealth and prosperity for its entire community. This real estate investment firm grew out of a real estate development business that had eighteen thousand housing units and more than twenty-six hundred investors. DLP stands for dream, live, prosper, and they are a faith- and mission-based organization that has the big goal of providing affordable housing for one million people. By licensing their internal operating platform—Elite Execution System—they help other real estate developers grow their businesses, which multiplies their impact.

ADVERTISE PURPLE

Results-based affiliate marketing agency (B2B)
Primary customer acquisition channel: outbound direct sales via cold calling

Advertise Purple, based in Santa Monica, California, is a marketing agency that provides affiliate marketing services to companies on a pay-for-performance basis, which means they help companies launch online affiliate marketing programs to increase sales through partner channels. They have grown 679 percent from 2018 to 2022 and have been honored with five consecutive years on the *Inc.* 5000 list. They have generated well over $3 billion in sales for their clients, for which they take a piece of the action. (An excellent business model!) A few years ago, they took a chance and invested in the development of their proprietary technology called Purply (gotta love that name), which accelerated their growth by helping them serve their customers better than their competitors. Beyond their data-driven approach and unique technology, their number-one growth lever is cold calling. (You thought it was dead, didn't you?) Kyle Mitnick told me about their approach:

> We're going to get out there and pound the pavement. Something that businesses today don't like to do and people don't like to do is cold calling. It is so taboo. But it's so effective. It's so uncomfortable yet so effective, and nobody wants to do it. Nobody talks about it. People think it's spammy. But the fact that very few organizations in our world do it gives us an inside track. And we're not selling here, we're consulting, and the way that we consult is simply giving anecdotes, by telling stories about clients that we've had in this prospects' vertical and how they did with us.

FREESTAR

Results-based programmatic ad agency (B2B)
Primary customer acquisition channel: outbound direct sales via cold calling

Freestar is a marketing agency that provides programmatic advertising on a revenue-share basis (similar to Advertise Purple) to any publisher or retailer that sells ads on their website. They have grown 700 percent from 2018 to 2022 and achieved their fourth consecutive listing on the *Inc.* 5000 list. They provide a platform backed by data science and engineering that increases publishers' ad revenue with a heavy focus on providing the best customer service ever seen in their industry (more on this later). Their founder is the consummate salesperson and started them on a path of direct sales with a cold-calling outreach process. As a digital marketing firm, you would think that that they would be experts in all things digital marketing, but their marketing leader told me that beyond their fantastic cold outreach sales efforts, their best customer acquisition return on investment (ROI) post-COVID-19 has been in-person events—specifically prospect dinners where the leadership team, customers, and prospects come together to discuss how publishers can increase their revenue. She emphasized that with so much digital everything, she believes there's a return to the human element. If she invested in only one growth lever, it would be in-person events.

FARMGIRL FLOWERS

E-commerce flowers (B2C)
Primary customer acquisition channel: Viral/organic social

Farmgirl Flowers is a direct-to-consumer floral e-commerce company. Since its founding, the company's annual revenue grew to more than $100 million. They are the only large-scale, female-founded, predominantly female-run e-commerce flower company. This structure gives them greater customer insight since the gifting and receiving of flowers is usually done by women for other women. They design the type of arrangements they want to receive themselves because they are the target customer. Launched in San Francisco in 2010 by founder and CEO Christina Stembel, their business model has been "You order. We pick. They're happy." This means that if you want to send extraordinary flowers to someone, let them figure it out—they've got your back! Farmgirl's number-one growth lever has been viral marketing. Their growth trajectory kicked into gear when they racked up hundreds of thousands of dollars for business expenses on the CapitalOne company credit card. CapitalOne dug into the company and found Christina, who became a spokesperson for CapitalOne, and this symbiotic relationship helped both companies grow rapidly. Most of all, they did a masterful job of growing by building an engaged community and partnerships, which I discuss in Part I. Kat Taylor Simonyi, head of North American operations for Farmgirl Flowers, described their thought process to me:

> It's something about how the product team works and how we approach business development because we are who we are because we're women. And then there's that connection to Christina [Farmgirl founder and CEO]. We haven't been able to spend a lot of money on customer acquisition because we don't have the money to spend on acquisition. We've instead invested in the quality of the products and what we put into the box, and then it's word of mouth.[12]

RETAIL SERVICE SYSTEMS (RSS)

Franchise development/mattress and home furniture (B2C)
Primary customer acquisition channel: partners/franchisees

RSS is a franchise development company with several direct-to-consumer brands (Dropbox mattresses, etc.) sold and distributed through a franchised dealer network. They have doubled their revenues almost every year since 2017 and have enjoyed five consecutive years on the *Inc.* 5000 list. They have been so successful at supporting their franchisees that 74 percent of the franchisees come from referrals from other franchisees. They have a patented sales method (didn't think you could do that, did you?), and their by-appointment-only model is so successful that they have a customer close rate higher than 90 percent. They use social media heavily to get customers in the door and closely track ROAS and CAC along with the sales metrics of bookings (show up, close rates, etc.) to make their franchisees more successful and profitable. Darren Conrad, executive vice president for RSS, told me about their differentiators:

> The difference between us and a retail store is significant. We create a sense of urgency and set up times to meet people. It's like selling something out of your garage. What's the benefit of that? Well, it creates an urgency. I can schedule times to meet people instead of sitting in the store. And I can do it in a three-hour window of time. So I can meet people every thirty minutes for three hours a day. And all I'm doing is meeting people when they're buying from me.[13]

CLICKFUNNELS

B2B software

Primary customer acquisition channel: paid ads and community

ClickFunnels was born in 2014 when the frustration and time required to build an online sales funnel became too challenging to make and manage. Cofounders Russell Brunson and Todd Dickerson got together for a week and mapped out their dream software, asking questions like, "Well, what if it could do this?" Todd built ClickFunnels in the months to follow, and

Russell sold it. In October 2014, Russell launched ClickFunnels with a small team and no VC funding. Since then, ClickFunnels has been one of North America's fastest-growing, privately owned SaaS companies, with more than $100 million in annual sales and more than one hundred thousand customers. ClickFunnels has grown 1,011 percent since 2016, or an average of 144 percent (more than doubling) every year for the past seven years. The company hit $160 million in revenue in December 2022 and supports more than 120,000 customers worldwide, making it one of the fastest-growing bootstrapped companies in the world. Russell is a prolific marketer and has expertly used the growth lever of self-liquidating advertising. This means they create low-cost, high-value offers that pay for the advertising spend. Any follow-on marketing of their core product offerings is pure gross profit. This customer acquisition strategy has generated the cash the company needed to continue growing.[14]

NP DIGITAL

Integrated marketing agency (B2B)
Primary customer acquisition channel: SEO and content development

Neil Patel and Mike Kamo cofounded NP Digital and its umbrella of digital marketing agencies. Neil Patel is a *New York Times* bestselling author, is recognized as a top influencer by the *Wall Street Journal*, and is a *Forbes* top-ten marketer. Mike Kamo is a leader in building, managing, and scaling businesses. NP Digital is one of the leaders in SEO and is an SEO company.

The history of NP Digital stretches back to when Neil started his first company at the age of sixteen. Having borrowed money from his parents to pay a marketing agency to help grow his business, Neil soon found himself without results and without money. It was a quick lesson that motivated Neil to learn everything he could about marketing and do it on his own. In late 2017, NP Digital was born. NP Digital has had impressive growth; it has tripled in revenue in the last couple of years, and its team size has also tripled and consists of more than 750 remote-first workers.[15]

Whenever one of my companies suggested we use a specific SEO agency to help us, I searched for that company on the web. Since they purport to be experts at SEO, they should come up on the first page of Google results. If they didn't, then they didn't get my business. For NP Digital, as we like to say in the technology business, they ate their own dog food. (What a weird saying.) In other words, they mastered for themselves what they do for their clients. As of this writing, if you search "SEO" on Google or Bing, Neil's agency comes up in the top ten organic search results.

PART I

Team

attract →
hire →
support →
grow →
release

I start this book by discussing how our BFGs build their high-performance teams because nothing else is more important than that. You can have a great strategy but a bad team, and you'll most likely fail, or at a minimum never reach your optimal organizational performance. Conversely, you can have a poor strategy and a great team, and eventually your team will figure it out.

Each of these BFG companies did an excellent job of attracting, hiring, and leading exceptional teams, but they all did it in their own unique way. As the war for talent continues to rage, there is nothing more important for CEOs and their teams to focus on than this function.

This part is broken down into five chapters corresponding to the major phases of building a team.

- Attract: strategizing about who to hire and then finding and recruiting top performers who are good fits for your culture
- Hire: avoiding hiring mistakes by selecting the right individuals and rejecting those who aren't
- Support: ensuring people stick around and perform at their highest levels
- Grow: building the next level of leadership
- Release: building a company run by the team or responsibly ushering them into new opportunities

Farmgirl Flowers experienced a level of bootstrapped growth other founders can only dream about. They grew from $2 million to $100 million in annual revenue in five years. Along the way, they developed a California distribution center, hired more than one hundred employees, and then summarily shut down the facility after discovering that it wasn't profitable. They made a ton of mistakes around hiring people but got better and better along the way. They have a very strong culture and are proud of being a bootstrapped company, which they emphasize in their interviews with prospects. They want every new employee to know that because they are bootstrapped, they (not VCs or bankers) are in control of their own destiny. They make their own decisions, and they move quickly.

Learning from what worked, they now employ an "employee experience manager" to ensure that every new employee matriculates effectively and has a superior onboarding experience. And because they have a lean team, each employee has the opportunity to make an impact. To save money and ensure that a new hire can add value, they require every first-line manager to have a thirty/sixty/ninety-day plan for their employee before creating a requisition for a new employee.

This is just one of the companies I highlight in this part, so if you want to recruit, hire, retain, and support a high-performing team to help reach your growth goals, then learn from companies like Farmgirl Flowers and the rest of our BFGs.

Chapter 1

ATTRACT

People are *not* your most important asset.
The *right* people are.

—JIM COLLINS, *GOOD TO GREAT*

KEY INSIGHTS

- Focus on discovering and effectively describing your culture before you hire.
- Spend as much time creating your ideal employee as you do your ideal customer.
- Focus on values, outcome-based skills, and culture fit only.
- Create compelling job descriptions and corresponding job ads/postings.

Finding and Attracting Culture-Fit Top Performers

Doubling revenue every year consistently like our BFGs have done requires different people doing different things as each new level of growth is reached (including serious personal growth by the CEO/founder). You'll have to make tough people choices, including letting go of certain team members as the growth outpaces their talents. During the interviews, I heard about plenty of tough choices that were made to dismiss early team members. No one I spoke with regretted those decisions, although almost every CEO said they wished they had done it sooner.

Your rate of growth is directly related to the quality of the people on the team. But finding the right people for a growing business has never been more challenging. Small businesses used to have the advantage of location over more prominent companies in major metropolitan areas; post-COVID-19, as the more prominent companies allow remote work, that advantage has gone away. The competition for top talent has never been tougher since big companies can now compete for the same talent anywhere in the world that small companies used to target.

Based on what has worked so well with our BFGs, I want to help you avoid many of the hiring mistakes they made. You can do this by putting the foundational elements in place *before* recruiting one person. I cover this in detail in the following sections, but you must first take these three steps:

1. Clarify and illuminate your culture.
2. Decide on the core traits/values that complement your culture, which you need in every person.
3. Detail the relevant skills per role that will drive the outcomes you are looking for.

Focus First on the "C" Word

Culture eats strategy for breakfast.
—LASZLO BOCK, *Work Rules!*

Your secret weapon to attracting the best and brightest is the "C" word. In fact, the "C" word is way more important than you think!

Each one of the BFGs focused heavily on building a unique culture that attracted specific types of people. From DLP Capital's focus as a faith-based organization to Farmgirl Flowers' celebration as a lean bootstrapped company to Advertise Purple's focus on fun, each one was able to identify what a "culture-fit" top performer looked like to them and then use various methods to attract them into their companies. Kyle Mitnick learned that Advertise Purple needed to be bold with their company culture, particularly when interacting with potential new hires: "Culture in recruiting was way more impactful than we thought—we needed culture on the walls and in the halls!"[1]

Yep, culture is that important.

The big idea in this section is to ensure that you understand and can articulate your culture before recruiting a new employee. This doesn't mean you slap together your mission statement and copy your values from someone else's website. You need to dig deep to determine the essence of your company and what you value most in your employees (and contractors) and consciously focus on building that culture. Don Wenner, founder and CEO of DLP Capital, explained that this is an ongoing and continuous process:

> Today, most people, especially in leadership seats, have done a significant amount of research prior to ever talking to you. That's why it's so important to first clearly define who you are, what you do, and what makes your culture. You have to invest in websites like Glassdoor,

> making it clear who you are. Encourage people to submit reviews. And most people understand the good, the bad, and the indifferent, right? The people that say negative things about us on a website like Glassdoor are probably as valuable, or more valuable, to a potential candidate to read than the positive things.[2]

Another way of thinking about culture is that you (and your team) need to be able to succinctly answer the following question: "What's it like to work here, and what's in it for me if I join?" And your answers should be fairly uniform and consistent.

Every one of the companies I interviewed could do this. It doesn't matter what your hiring model is; you need to be able to answer that question completely and consistently. For instance, JCW and Advertise Purple primarily hire college graduates and focus on the professional growth they can obtain, Dribbble seeks those who are a "culture-add," not a "culture-fit." In all cases, they can answer that question for their target candidates.

Megan Crutcher and Justin Ring, the cofounders of Odyssey Engineering Group, stated that culture is their most significant factor in hiring, especially when hiring people from their competitors.[3] Their culture is very defined and strategically very different than their competition. They preach work-life balance and go so far as to *require* employees to work only forty hours a week. This is one of their biggest differentiators, and everyone seems to stick to that. Despite what you may think about that policy as a company leader, they have experienced incredible growth.

Dribbble's first step in their interviewing process is to assess culture fit (and the basics—salary, timing, etc.). Aasha Anam, the former global head of talent acquisition for JCW Group, told us they have Culture Champions in each regional office who are responsible for ensuring that the company culture is nurtured.[4]

Freestar takes this so seriously that they assess, monitor, and recognize people against their Culture Index. Robert Brill, the CEO of Brill Media, places an enormous emphasis on culture: "Culture is everything—the heart and soul—learning, respect, empathy, peers, committed, passionate, enthusiastic. This is what we look for."[5]

Today's employees hold elevated expectations of their employers—expectations that extend beyond financial compensation. A recent LinkedIn survey revealed that 65 percent of individuals are willing to accept lower compensation and 26 percent are willing to forgo prestigious job titles rather than endure an unsatisfactory workplace environment. Candidates actively seek workplaces where their values align with the company's mission.[6] Lindsey Whalen Draska, former head of people and culture at Farmgirl Flowers, has firsthand experience with this:

> I think since 2020, culture has been one of the top items that candidates come into organizations wanting to know about and how they'll experience it from day one. And I think that is an amazing expectation. Gone are the days when people come in and they're like well, we'll just see how I fit in. That doesn't happen anymore.[7]

Understanding your culture and explaining it to potential new hires takes time and effort. It requires being honest about the firm's culture, both the positives and the negatives. Jonathan Moisan, CEO of Advertise Purple, describes the lengths they go to when talking with a potential new hire:

> Spending that hour talking with someone and explaining to them, hey, in this culture, these are the type of

> things and challenges you're going to face. We're very upfront from the beginning and that allows us to demonstrate the honesty of both our shortcomings and our successes. This makes a candidate feel comfortable that they are joining a company where they know exactly what they are getting themselves into. I feel like a lot of companies paint this picture that it's all rainbows and butterflies, and then all of a sudden, they start day one and they end up saying this is the worst job ever.[8]

In our search to understand how these companies could attract such outstanding teams, we scoured the 324 fastest-growing companies' websites to look for how they described their cultures and whether they were compelling enough (in our opinion) to attract culture-fit candidates.

The following are descriptions of company culture from our group of BFGs that I believe would attract the best candidates. I also include a few bad ones as a contrast and remove the company names to protect the guilty. Would you consider working for these companies?

Capital Brand Group

> Warrior Spirit—you work hard, embrace adversity, operate with a high sense of urgency, solve problems, and find solutions. Your teammates can rely on you to carry your share of the load; you demonstrate consistently strong performance, and you aggressively pursue growth.
>
> Servant's Heart—you place the needs of others above your own and you encourage others at every opportunity. You treat people with respect independent of their status or disagreement with you. You are humble and ego-less when searching for the best solutions.

> You make time to develop others by teaching, coaching, and helping your colleagues.
>
> A Positive Attitude—you don't take yourself too seriously; you keep morale high; you inspire others with desire for excellence; you celebrate wins in a rewarding work environment; you are passionate, and most importantly, you have fun![9]

In stark contrast to Capital Brand Group's very specific description of their culture, here's an example from a company that will remain unnamed. If you join this unnamed company, you will be part of a "community of like-minded professionals looking for exceptional career opportunities and growth. We are hyper-focused on creating value-adding experiences for top talent worldwide."

Which statement gives you a better sense of the company you would be joining? Which one generates more excitement? The eloquence of Capital Brand Group's statement is much more likely to attract top performers.

PRX Performance

> Think Big: Led by creativity and innovation, we recognize the opportunities standing in front of us today are a direct correlation of our ability to dream and believe.
>
> Service our customers above all else: We have a great desire to provide the highest quality products paired with an unforgettable customer experience. We are committed to achieving the level of excellence all of our customers deserve. They are our #1 priority. If they are not satisfied, we're not either. . . .
>
> Do the Right Thing: We believe that a culture of openness and humility is the pathway to achieving

> PRs, both personally and professionally. We strive to be intellectually honest and act with integrity in everyday business and life. We are committed to doing the right thing for the right reasons and upholding our values in every decision.[10]

Contrast this with a statement from another unnamed company: "Innovate and exceed the needs of customers." Whew. How inspiring. Which company would you prefer to work for?

Pendo

> Pendo culture combines the thrill of a startup with the reassurance of grown-up responsibility. At our core, we're a team of resourceful individuals who love to question everything. But where some companies may fail to focus that energetic, rebellious streak, Pendozers channel our collective bias to act into innovation, colorful (pink!) celebrations, and a maniacal focus on our customers. Our teams are fiercely loyal, independent, and fun loving, so be prepared for a helping of honest, direct feedback from a team that wants to see you thrive.[11]

Pendo is a dynamic company, and their statement conveys that vividly. Contrast their statement with this one from a different company, where "you can expect a dynamic and driven work environment. To foster your success, you will be surrounded by a positive and supportive culture that encourages everyone to help develop themselves and others." That one falls flat and is devoid of energy, whereas Pendo's statement pulls me out of my chair and infuses me with energy. Where would you rather work?

ShipBob

> We believe everything is achievable. As we tackle challenges across the supply chain, we have the opportunity to stretch, learn, grow, and blaze a new path. This environment is a place where you can take risks and be empowered to do the best work of your career.
>
> With an expansive network, we are surrounded by resilient entrepreneurs and creative problem-solvers from diverse cultures that are united in their commitment of service to the global community through trust, feedback, and common purpose.
>
> We are stronger, more resilient, and more creative through transparency. Our best solutions can come from anywhere if we are all aligned on the same mission. With this belief, everyone at ShipBob adopts an ownership mindset with an all-hands-on-deck approach.[12]

ShipBob has a strong focus on risk-taking, problem-solving, common purpose, and transparency, and those attributes come through in their statement. In contrast, this statement from a firm I won't identify includes similar positive attributes but lacks the specificity and energy of ShipBob's statement: "Always prioritizing excellence, fairness, and quality in everything we do, we are committed to engaging honestly and fairly with everyone, maintaining a level of service beyond what is expected, and continuously improving the quality of everything we do as a team." This statement tells me almost nothing about the actual culture at their company.

Dribbble

> A culture of communication, collaboration, & connection. We've been fully remote since day one, and are

> building a fully distributed team across North America. We believe that creative collaboration can happen anywhere, and that working remotely shouldn't have to mean sacrificing a sense of cohesion, community, and connection. We've seen that by combining thoughtful collaboration, frequent communication, and the freedom for people to be their authentic selves, you can do your best work and inspire others to do the same.[13]

Dribbble's statement focuses on their connections and collaboration. Their statement presents a stark contrast with a firm that is, perhaps, just a little too old-fashioned in their calm and bland description of their company culture: "We are focused on creating value. Call us old-fashioned, but we believe that trust isn't just given. It is earned. It's about building relationships. Building solutions and approaching every project as unique. Most importantly, we are about family, and our family works night and day to create value for yours."

GenTech

> At GenTech, we uphold that investing in our people is investing in our business. You'll never be just another face in the crowd here. We encourage growth, emphasize teamwork, and promote opportunity. Connection and accountability are high on our list of values, as is rewarding a job well done. . . . We choose to be pioneers because "we've always done it this way" doesn't resonate with us. The innovators at GenTech work together to find new ideas that become new practices. They invent new methods to analyze data. They study robotics and reimagine systems. You will have the freedom to nurture

> your innovative spirit here; and with a little work, an opportunity to bring your ideas to life.[14]

GenTech's statement is suffused with energy and avoids platitudes. Contrast this with another statement from a company: "Mutual trust and transparency between teams enable seamless collaboration. We ensure honesty and fairness. One of the key factors that drives excellence and innovation is an analytical approach. Having a sense of urgency is what helps us in getting a lot done within a short period of time." A place that says they have a sense of urgency has a statement that is lulling me to sleep. The lack of self-reflection is apparent in the lackluster company statement.

I think you can see the stark differences between the companies that have figured out what they are all about and can articulate it in a compelling way, and those who haven't. If you want to attract the best candidates, you must sell your company by painting a compelling and accurate picture of what it's like to work for your company.

The Core Values and Traits of Top-Performing Teams

Core values are essential for enduring greatness, but it doesn't seem to matter what those core values are.

—JIM COLLINS, *Good to Great*

Once you create and describe your culture and identify precisely what a culture-fit employee looks like, you must define what core traits and values will complement your culture. You must be able to quantifiably determine whether a new employee has those attributes. This assessment should be addressed during the hiring process (which I cover in the next chapter). For instance, JCW looks to hire "hungry learners," and in fact, they go so far as to give them books to read on their birthday.

We looked at every one of our 324 BFGs' websites to identify the top traits they require when hiring people. This doesn't mean that if you also look for these same characteristics, you're guaranteed success. But in my experience, and in the interviews I conducted, if you create a recruiting and hiring process that attracts the right culture-fit people and hire for the core personality traits required for the role, you'll build a high-performance team. Being clear about your company's values and culture helps you attract the right people. As Bobby Frazitta, senior vice president of people and culture from RIVA Solutions, put it, "I think nowadays people are really looking for a place that aligns with who they are as a person."[15]

The following list represents the most frequently mentioned traits across the 324 BFG companies in order of frequency of mentions from most to least:

1. Passion/passionate
2. Team/teamwork
3. Customer-focused
4. Helping others/collaborative
5. Driven/motivated
6. Talented
7. Industry-specific skills
8. Creative
9. Positive
10. Integrity
11. Fun
12. Challenge (the status quo)

13. Smart
14. Dynamic
15. Committed
16. Diverse
17. Respect
18. Attitude
19. Innovative
20. Excellence

In addition to looking for traits that align with their mission and culture, many of the BFGs I interviewed conduct individual performance reviews to assess performance around their core values. Here are a few more characteristic traits from our BFGs:

- JCW: grit, growth, greatness
- Dribbble: help customers succeed, take action, deliver results, bring good vibes
- Freestar: customer (publisher) first; above and beyond; we, not me
- RIVA: results, innovation, values, accountability
- Advertise Purple: collaborative, fun, hard-working, intelligent, open door

Based on our collective analysis of all the BFGs, the following six traits are vital for hiring the right people to drive a fast-growing company. Of course, you might care about some of these core traits more than others, depending on the job. Your company is unique, so you should look for traits that make someone great at their job in your business. I'm not suggesting that only hiring for these values will ensure your success and faster growth, but I don't think you can go wrong if you model what the BFGs value the most.

1. *Grit:* Things move quickly in the world of fast-growing companies, and jobs can be unclear. The right team members must handle new jobs and figure things out as they go, even if it gets repetitive. You want people who don't give up easily.
2. *Accountability:* Team members should do what they say they're going to do. You can't afford to constantly check in with people to see whether they have completed a job, so this trait is paramount.
3. *Impact:* Impact means making a real difference at work. You want people who understand the company's goals and work the right way to meet them.
4. *Teamwork:* Workplaces have all kinds of people, and companies are becoming more global. Good team players understand and care about others.
5. *Ownership:* This means taking charge when things go wrong and not just complaining. You're looking for people who fix problems and keep going.
6. *Curiosity:* The world is changing fast, so you want lifelong learners who have no ego and want to figure things out.

But before recruiting any new employee, assess whether you *really* need that new employee!

It's easy to give in to employees who are complaining about too much work and saying that you need more staff. But before you post that job opening, see whether you can realign or eliminate tasks, promote from within, or outsource that function. Measure your sales or profit per employee compared to your industry, and this will help you assess whether you are over or understaffed.

This seems like common sense, but every one of the BFGs I spent time with was very lean, considering their size and growth rates. They made hiring decisions very judiciously. This helped them save cash and ensured that every new person hired was given special attention to ensure their success. This sounds like a no-brainer, but it's pretty easy to give in to the calls of overwhelm and quickly post a new job announcement. Companies rarely press pause to see whether they have options other than hiring a new team member.

For instance, sometimes it might be better to hire a specialist with a unique set of skills instead of waiting for an employee's skill set to develop internally. It may be more suitable to engage a freelance expert to resolve the problem instead of bringing in a full-time employee. I did this frequently at my consulting firm. We only hired full-time for what we considered "core skills," and we found freelancers and independent consultants to fill the roles of highly specialized skills.

Hiring on-demand teams to help grow and scale through many freelance sites has never been easier. That's why this part is called "Team" and not "Employees."

It's essential to think holistically about how you grow more profitably with less stress on cash and hiring for culture-add. Think about what will serve the organization in the immediate and distant future.

Also, screen your consultants and freelancers against your culture and values! Most companies look for someone with a specific skill set to get the job done, but adding the additional culture-fit screening criteria may offer you fewer issues with any and all external team members!

> Check out our Book Resources section at www.scaleupfaster.com/resources to see how you can use our AI-based platform to dramatically improve your profit-per-employee ratio as you grow and scale.

Create the Profile of a Dream Employee

Now that you have described your culture and identified the key character traits you are looking for, it's time to start putting together your candidate package. Like our BFGs, start with describing in detail the ideal type of person that would be a great culture fit and addition to your team. Be careful not to define the perfect employee, but describe a person who fits the culture, aligns with your values, and has the core skills to achieve the desired outcomes of the job.

It's astounding how many companies will take the time to create a detailed avatar or persona of their ideal customer but not the perfect employee. Many books have been written about the idea that by focusing on your employees first, they will take care of your customers. I believe this, too, which is why you should define your ideal employee profile (IEP), which combines the culture fit, core values, and general skills needed for every job in your company.

In my previous consulting firm, my cofounder and I created a manifesto that described the ideal type of people we wanted to work with, what values we needed them to hold dear, and what kind of culture we wanted—before we hired a single employee. When we surveyed our employees after our fifth anniversary, asking them to describe our company values for our new website, it was almost exactly what we had laid out in our manifesto. By focusing on this in our earliest days, we had a 92 percent voluntary retention rate over nine years.

The ideal profile for our BFGs varied widely. Each company had different cultures and hiring models. For instance, look at how different the profiles of ideal candidates are for some of our BFGs:

- JCW: They only hire new college grads for their recruiting roles.
- Advertise Purple: They look for people from the top schools who have a high GPA, are involved in extracurricular activities, are enthusiastic, and are highly intelligent.

- Dribbble: They poach most of their people from competitors and pay them higher than the industry average through bonuses based on company performance.
- DLP Capital: They look for leadership potential. Their motto is "Leaders are made here."
- Retail Service Systems: They have to be hungry and have an internal drive.
- Freestar: Intelligent problem-solvers who own the outcome. No toxic people.
- Farmgirl Flowers: They take personal responsibility. They're gutsy, principled, raw, and open to learning. They want people who can make a strategic impact and are innovative.

Check out our Book R\esources section at www.scaleupfaster.com/resources for example ideal employee profiles (IEP) to model.

Identify the Outcome-Based Skills Needed for the Role

I want everyone to come to work on a Monday morning tapping into their natural self.

—AASHA ANAM, former global head of talent acquisition for JCW Group

The resume is dead. Stop focusing on it.

Not only are resumes lousy predictors of job success, but so is education level and, to some degree, experience. This is because resumes often fail to identify the most skilled applicants for a role. It can be challenging to assess whether a resume is accurate and even more difficult to determine the applicants' actual skills using resumes.

Instead of the resume, focus on the skills needed to be successful in the job—the skills you can objectively measure. Companies that concentrate on skills-based hiring versus resumes stated the following in a recent survey:[16]

- 91.9 percent of employers believe skills-based hiring is more effective for identifying talented candidates than resumes.
- 88.8 percent of employers believe that skills-based hiring is more predictive of on-job success than resumes.
- 81.8 percent of employers believe that employees hired via skills-based hiring stay longer.

Employers that adopted a skills-based hiring approach achieved the following business results:[17]

- 88 percent reduced mis-hires
- 88 percent improved diversity
- 74 percent reduced cost to hire
- 82 percent reduced total time to hire
- 89 percent increased employee retention

Many candidates who lack degree qualifications can still develop the necessary skills for the job through relevant work experience and self-study. This is especially true for entry-level positions.

New technical skills are constantly emerging, especially in fast-evolving fields like software development. Four-year degrees simply can't keep up with this rate of change. If hiring top talent is a priority, skills-based hiring must replace resume screening. By forgoing resumes and putting skills-based hiring first, "employers ensure that only those candidates with the right hard and soft skills, cognitive abilities, and culture add are passed through the screening stage to subsequent rounds. Skills-based hiring is a cornerstone in the new world of work."[18]

Develop Compelling Job Descriptions for the Specific Roles

Be sure to detail in the job ad, position description, and application process what culture-fit looks like, compensation range, location, citizenship, et cetera. Also describe the hiring process and general timing so that a candidate who is desperate and needs a job before you are ready to make a decision opts out of the process.

—LINDSEY WHALEN DRASKA, former head of people and culture at Farmgirl Flowers

The initial misstep in the hiring process often occurs right at the beginning, when crafting the job description. Many companies take the lazy route and simply copy and paste someone else's job description, or just as bad, let ChatGPT do it. There's nothing wrong with starting there, but if that's where the effort ends, you'll never attract the best candidates.

The job description is advertising your company, even though very few people view it that way, so let your culture shine through. Detail how high performance is achieved and is based on outcomes, not experience or education. Top performers will be attracted to this type of description, and low performers will self-select out.

People yearn to make meaningful contributions and to feel invigorated and passionate about their work. They seek inspiration from ideas that can address challenges and fulfill needs. This doesn't necessarily entail changing the world or tackling grandiose issues. Instead, it means believing that one is making a positive impact, even in a small yet significant manner within their sphere of influence.

Organizations must ensure that the roles they're recruiting for offer opportunities for meaningful work, personal development, and impact. This message should be conveyed through the job description and during the interview process, but it begins well before you start a specific hiring process. Communicating your company's culture and identity, which is a key part of bringing on the *right* new hires, is an ongoing process.

Hiring individuals whose values align with your organization's mission becomes a mutually beneficial arrangement. Craft your job description in a manner that entices such candidates to apply. When you get the job description right, you're offering your next employee the opportunity to embrace market risk—to explore uncharted territory within your organization and leverage their unique strengths. Finding the right fit means allowing your new hire to flourish; as your employees grow, so does your organization.

What follows is an example of a great outcome and culture-based job description that will attract the right kind of person.

Job title: Waiter
Manager: Sarah Smith
Team: Front of house

Key objectives for new hire

- Improve customer service at My French Restaurant
- Decrease customer wait times at My French Restaurant

Measurable outcomes

- Increase the number of tables we turn over each night

- Decrease the number of complaints on social media and feedback forms
- Increase the number of positive reviews on social media and feedback forms

The ideal candidate will have the following:

Skills and experience:

- Customer service skills
- Experience dealing with customer complaints
- Cleaning/bussing skills
- Organizational skills
- Tech skills to work ordering systems/tills
- Experience waiting tables

Personality traits:

- Outgoing
- Friendly
- Warm
- Professional
- Remains calm in stressful situations
- Can think on their feet
- Cooperative
- Hard-working

Cultural aspects:

- Enjoys French food

- Knowledge of French cuisine
- Knowledge of French culture
- Enjoys socializing
- Enjoys team bonding exercises

See how clear that is? This job description may repel some candidates (which is good) and should attract more of the right candidates!

Develop an Exceptional Candidate Experience

After identifying and articulating your culture, consider the candidate's journey. Start by putting yourself in the candidate's shoes. Top-performing employees have plenty of options for where to work, so if you understand the candidate's journey, you'll create a better experience and attract better candidates. What follows is an example of the journey a top candidate might take.

Meet Heidi, our hypothetical job seeker, as she begins her quest to join your company. Heidi, already familiar with your organization's mission and values through social media (LinkedIn, Instagram), stumbles upon a job ad for an enticing role.

Before applying, she briefly explores Glassdoor, seeking confirmation that your company garners glowing reviews and is renowned as a fantastic workplace. Heidi revisits your social media accounts, noting posts celebrating employee milestones and your accomplishments. Satisfied, she returns to the job ad, ready to start a straightforward application process.

Throughout her application, your hiring team maintains open communication with Heidi, keeping her informed and engaged. She understands the application process because it is well communicated on your website, so she always knows where she is in the process. She knows what's in it for her if she works for your company, and the prospect of joining your team fills her with enthusiasm.

After the interviews, assessments, and reference checks, it is clear that Heidi is the standout candidate. She successfully secures the position.

In Heidi's journey, numerous touchpoints contributed to her decision to apply for the position and ultimately join your team. Let's delve into the five pivotal components shaping a candidate's experience, whether positively or negatively.

THE JOB POSTING

Develop a compelling job posting using an outcome and values-based job description for the specific role. Your job posting should do more than inform; it should ignite excitement in potential candidates. After reading it, applicants should believe they can excel in the role and aspire to be part of your organization for years. The job posting should answer this question: What's it like to work here, and what's in it for me if I do?

JCW does a great job of describing the career paths, timing, and compensation for all roles—just take a look at the Careers page of their website.

EMPLOYER BRANDING

Building your employer brand significantly influences the candidate's experience. Your employer brand encompasses your company's reputation, which is evident through your social media presence, career pages, and online reputation. Candidates research you on Google and social media to form an impression of your company. RIVA does an outstanding job of giving candidates a peek into what it's like to work there through their extensive postings on LinkedIn.

THE APPLICATION

In today's world, top candidates won't invest hours applying for a job. Streamline your application process and make it quick, engaging, and user-friendly. Lengthy applications deter high-quality candidates.

THE HIRING PROCESS

Selecting the right candidate is a challenge, so aim to minimize the number of interviews, tests, and assessments; pare those down to the essentials. Prolonged selection processes can deter candidates, and the competition may snatch your preferred choice before you extend an offer. I cover this more in the next chapter.

THE OFFER PROCESS

Extending an offer is a pivotal moment that sets the tone for the candidate's on-the-job experience. Transparent communication about salary expectations from the start is essential. Ensure fairness by providing candidates with salary range information throughout the recruitment journey to prevent disillusionment.

Here are some additional tips:

- Create an ad and/or a recruiting event that will generate enough traffic to attract the right candidates.
- Be different and have fun creating unique ways to show potential job seekers what it's truly like to work for your company.
- Use video to help candidates visualize working for your company.
- Describe the interviewing process in the job description.
- Be sure to include social proof by highlighting your employees (no stock photos of a diverse group of happy people, please!) through your website and social channels like LinkedIn.

- Tap into your current employees through an attractive employee referral program.

Beware the Experienced Hire

Many of the BFGs I talked to tried and failed at hiring experienced people. I had the same experience in my company. It's not that the people we hired from the more prominent companies were not competent. It's that we didn't effectively screen them for culture fit. Just because someone worked for a more prominent company than yours in a similar job doesn't mean they will/can do the work necessary to succeed in your environment. Constantly objectively evaluate how they will work out in a smaller company.

The primary reason for the additional scrutiny of an experienced hire is that it's virtually impossible to separate the brand equity that accrues to an individual working for a large firm independently from their success. For instance, it's pretty easy for a person who works for a company like IBM (where I used to work) to get a meeting, but not so easy for "Pete's brand new little consulting firm." You should explore this during the interview process, as DLP Capital does. They ask about the context in which potential hires were working to find out what factors contributed to their success. They ask the candidates about the resources available to them and the stage of growth the business was in (retracting versus scrappy start-up). Different measures of success apply based on the business stage and speed of growth.

Your Remote/Work-from-Home Policy

When this book was written, the debate on whether companies should allow employees to work from home was raging. COVID-19 accelerated working from home since many people couldn't be on site, but many people didn't want to return to the office once the COVID-19–era restrictions were lifted.

This benefitted most of our BFGs (and still does), because they were either primarily remote or considering moving in that direction before COVID-19 hit. They believed that a culture built on creating an environment for supporting remote employees was a competitive advantage that attracted great employees, so they made recruiting and hiring processes to support this strategy. For instance, because Dribbble was a 100 percent remote company from its founding, they look for people who are very articulate and communicative (orally and in writing) because those skills are critical for working with others remotely.

A few companies had policies requiring two to three days in the office but were very purposeful in their policies. They reinforced that remote/home time is quiet work time to focus on getting tasks done and office time is meeting time. They found that sticking to those policies improved employee morale and productivity. Chloe Oddleifson, former vice president of operations at Dribbble, explained the myriad benefits of their work-from-home policy:

> We believe that remote is the best way to set people up for success in working where they can feel most inspired, most comfortable, and most productive. But we firmly believe that being a remote team shouldn't preclude us feeling connected to one another. So there's no need for us to feel isolated or like we're working on an island. We believe that done correctly, remote can foster this sense of community and connection and collaboration and communication. No one's talking about the two hours of your day that you missed with your two-year-old when they started

> to learn how to walk when you were commuting into the office or no one's talking about, you know, the lunch that you could have just like popped out and seen your kid, but instead you're in the office. I think there's a huge element about culture where we can live our lives more fully because of where we work. I am home every single day when my husband gets home from work, we're able to chat and connect, and then it's okay if I go back to work. I want to have kids someday, and working remotely gives me the freedom to know that I'll be able to be a much more involved parent. I'll be able to be present, but I'll also be able to have a job. I think for women now that is powerful, because a couple decades ago, it was either you're in an office away from your kid or you're at home. You're not modeling what it could look like to have a career and your children. It's a tradeoff we don't have to make anymore.[19]

Chloe is describing the enormous competitive advantages of a flexible work environment. If your company has not adopted this attitude, it is probably missing out on some high-quality hires.

Chapter 2

HIRE

The best thing you can do for employees—a perk better than foosball or free sushi—is hire only "A" players to work alongside them.

—VERNE HARNISH, *SCALING UP*

KEY INSIGHTS

- Interview/screen for culture fit (values) first, fundamental competencies/skills second, and evidence of producing job outcomes third.
- Create a hiring process that resembles the job to be done.
- Stop trusting your gut—it's usually wrong.
- Hire for potential/train for specific skills!
- Use tests and assessments (including AI-based systems) strategically, but don't over-rely on them.

There are multiple objectives when taking candidates through an interviewing/hiring process, including the following:

- Weeding out the candidates who are not good fits for the company or role.
- Solidifying the interest of candidates who are a good fit for the company and role.
- Branding the company to any or all potential candidates (and your competitors and partners).

No number of assessments, tests, interviews, or reference checks will keep you from making a bad hire, but taking some lessons from our BFGs will, I hope, improve your success rate at hiring top performers for your company. Lord knows I've made many hiring mistakes where I trusted my gut rather than following an objective hiring process—only to get gut-punched later when the hire turned into a disaster. (And yep, I've done this more than once.) Even companies equipped with a well-structured hiring process can falter if they neglect to reassess how they evaluate candidates during the crucial screening phase.

My former business partner Nick used to ask me a critically important question: "When are we going to stop making hiring mistakes?" This question came after a bad hire that cost us tens of thousands of dollars. My response was that when we figure that out, we'll be billionaires because no one has figured it out completely.

I discovered this in my BFG interviews as well. I heard many stories of hiring mistakes that set the BFGs back significantly. But, in each case, they licked their wounds, figured out what went wrong, improved their process, and kept moving forward and getting better.

You've probably read the statistics about making a bad hire. Industry data paints a stark picture, suggesting that the financial toll of a bad hire can soar into the tens of thousands of dollars. The number of mis-hires across so many companies prompts a fundamental question: Is there truly an overabundance of bad apples lurking within the job market? (I hear this repeatedly from business leaders.)

The unequivocal answer is no.

More often than not, the culprit isn't the caliber of individuals entering the workforce but rather an inadequate, or absent, hiring process. In the absence of a structured and well-defined hiring process, many business leaders resort to relying on their instincts and intuition.

Stop doing that!

In his groundbreaking work presented in the book *Work Rules!*, Laszlo Bock, former senior vice president of people operations for Google, discovered that managers' gut and intuition are usually wrong. According to Bock, it's crucial not to rely solely on your instinct because our innate biases and preconceived notions often lead us astray. He found that a comprehensive work sample test is the most reliable barometer for gauging a candidate's suitability. In other words, test candidates on the work (outcomes) they will be asked to do. Following closely behind are evaluations of a candidate's general cognitive ability and, last, a structured interview, preferably behavioral or situational in nature.[1]

The interview process should leave little doubt about how the candidate will perform once they become an integral part of your team! If you have completed the hiring/interviewing process for the candidate and are still unsure whether they are the right fit, look at your process!

This doesn't require a ton of work or investment. For instance, Ellen Hughes, the office manager for Odyssey Engineering Group, which designs sophisticated water and sewer systems, described the engineering test they developed for potential new hires:

> Our hiring manager sits with a candidate and says, okay, here's a map of this area, and next to this street, draw me a water line. Now draw me a sewer line. Even if the candidate doesn't know the intricacies of water

> and sewer systems, we get to see what questions they ask and how they think.[2]

It can be that simple to create a practical, situational test.

Know that getting the hiring process right is like the Lexus slogan, "The Pursuit of Excellence." You'll never get it right all the time, and you need to keep working on it to improve, particularly as candidates' needs change and technology changes.

The general hiring process used by most of the BFGs is detailed in the following paragraphs. I found it to be very time-and-resource efficient. Since every one of the BFGs was lean, they needed to make sure that each step of the process filtered candidates in or out appropriately and made good use of the time spent by every employee involved in the process.

Prescreen. This is usually done on a candidate self-serve basis and often through a selfie video answering a basic set of questions. The goal is to secure the basic prequalifying information (role, salary, timing, location, fit) and do so at scale. According to Lindsey Whalen Draska, they have everyone submit a selfie video interview to answer the basic questions.

Assess cultural fit. This can be done by an internal or external recruiter based on a specific set of cultural-fit questions.

Evaluate core competencies/skills. The hiring manager usually completes this.

Qualify role-based skills and success at driving job outcomes. This is done by a team conducting behavioral interviews and/or assessments during an interview.

Executive interview (vice president, etc.). This was toward the end of the process for every company I spoke with, and the primary purpose was to give the candidate the ability to ask questions about the company, culture, and other attributes. This was also a big test to determine how prepared and engaged the candidate was.

Reference checks. After a conditional offer, the HR or similar team will conduct the reference checks. It's important to be sure the candidate would accept the offer if an offer is made, so that no time is wasted doing reference checks if the candidate isn't going to accept.

Now let's look at each step of the process in detail.

Prescreen

We do an HR screen first before it gets to a hiring manager. . . . You can tell if someone is engaged, if they're excited, if they're, ready to learn, just from the way they answer some of the questions, like if they're really looking for a new challenge, a new opportunity.

—**CHRISTY ROSENSTEEL, general counsel and chief people officer for Freestar**

This step aims to quickly and efficiently eliminate anyone who is not a good fit. This is not designed to sell the right candidate for the company or position; it's to eliminate the ones who will be a time suck so you can focus on the most promising candidates who will be the best fit for your company. Aasha Anam explained to me that they frame their prescreen process around a number of key questions, like these: Do they want the job? Can they do the job? Do they have the right to work? Do they live a commutable distance? Can they speak the language? Have they done any research already? Do they understand what the job entails? Do they know what it is? What are their motivations? Do they align with what we offer? Can they do the job here?

This step of the process can be automated or outsourced to third-party recruiters or service providers. You want to know that the candidate is a good culture fit, has proper salary expectations, and meets any other critical requirements. The best strategy is to detail these items in the job ad itself, so your pre-screen ensures no one slips through who doesn't meet your standards. Let them self-select out if they are not a good fit.

Lindsey Whalen Draska told me they streamline their process by using a pre-recorded video explaining their first step. Their video welcomes the candidate, tells them they're going to be interviewed, and tells them what Farmgirl Flowers is looking for in their candidates. Then they ask the candidates to record their own two-minute video answering a few specified questions. As Lindsey explains, submitting a video is simply part of the application process, and if a candidate doesn't do it, they are immediately disqualified. It helps the hiring managers get to the know the candidate and provides information they can ask about during the in-person interviews. Lindsey noted that "It's very uncomfortable doing the video when people are not used to it. They don't really love it, but if they want the job, they have to do it."

Find the process that works for you and follow. Just like they do at Farmgirl Flowers.

Check for Cultural Fit

We, not me. . . . It's not my garbage or your garbage.
It's our garbage.
—CHRISTY ROSENSTEEL, Freestar

The second step in your hiring process should be to evaluate the candidate for cultural fit. Assuming that you have done an excellent job defining your company culture, you should be able to clearly articulate it—the personality of your company. Is it engineering-minded and serious? Is it fun and light? Do you subscribe to the work hard–party hard approach?

Some people will fit well with *any* culture, but you *must* have a process to ensure that the people who best fit the culture will be the ones who make it through the front end of the process. And you need to ensure that the ones who won't fit in get eliminated. Jonathan Moisan described their hiring process as one that is upfront and honest from the very beginning about their culture—including both their shortcomings and their successes. He said it gives candidates confidence that they know exactly what kind of company they would be joining. Jonathan contrasted Advertise Purple's approach with that of other companies: "I feel like a lot of companies paint this picture that it's all rainbows and butterflies and then all of a sudden the candidate starts on day one and they're saying this is the worst job ever." You can't let that happen.

At Dribbble, they follow a process where the internal (or external) recruiter assesses a candidate for culture first, as well as the basics (availability, salary expectations, etc.). If candidates pass the culture test, they move on to the hiring manager for an outcome-based interview.

Evaluate Core Competencies/Skills/Traits

In the realm of hiring, where much of the evaluation process hinges on the inherently subjective nature of interviews, it becomes imperative to implement measures that standardize qualitative feedback and responses as much as possible.

Freestar uses a "skills screen" because they want to hire for potential, and then they'll train for the specific skills required for a particular role. Christy Rosensteel, general counsel and chief people officer for Freestar, told me more about their skills screening process, which they use to verify whether candidates really have the skills they claim to have. She said, "We don't just want them to tell us that they can do this; *we want them to show us.*"[3] Rosensteel went on to explain that they might decide to hire a candidate who didn't pass the skills screen, but in such cases, because of their detailed process, the hiring managers are confident they aren't misled about a candidate's qualifications and abilities. In the end, Rosensteel said, their skills screen helps them hire based on the potential of the candidate.

Defining the qualities you value most is the first step toward consistent measurement. Remember that this process may take time and effort, but it's a valuable investment. Create a consistent hiring rubric describing what is a "1" versus a "2." Create objective criteria for defining 1–5 on a given trait/skill.

Once you've identified the core personality traits and competencies you desire in every candidate, everyone involved in the interview process must understand these criteria. Take the time to clearly explain terms like "ownership" and "grit," and make sure your team grasps their significance and can objectively assess whether a candidate has that competency at the level you desire. Aasha Anam told me that they look for three key personality traits: grit or resilience, a growth mindset, and natural curiosity. Aasha's team has a shared understanding of what they mean by those terms.

After conducting interviews, come together to review and adjust your evaluations of the candidates to maintain consistency. Also, be clear about what aspects of cultural fit or skills are mandatory and which ones can be learned.

In their quest to acquire top-tier talent, every growing company competes fiercely with big companies and is often unable to match their compensation and benefits packages. So, for smaller companies to compete for top talent, it becomes crucial to identify the qualities and competencies that truly matter and create a hiring rubric for uncovering them.

For instance, with only a few exceptions, the BFG companies place a premium on attributes like grit over conventional academic metrics (which college the candidate graduated from, their GPA, etc.). By focusing on core skills and competencies, your candidate pool expands significantly, and you get an edge on the competition for top talent over the traditional large companies that recruit heavily from the top schools.

Check out our Book Resources section at www.scaleupfaster.com/resources for sample interview questions that focus on core skills and outcome-based competencies.

Define the Role-Based Skills Needed to Drive Successful Job Outcomes

I've seen too many job descriptions and ads that include an exhaustive list of what a person must do in the new role. The candidate might need to do many things in their day-to-day function, but prior experience with those tasks may have little to do with their ultimate success in the role.

In your position description, focus on the *truly* critical job skills and competencies someone needs that result in specific outcomes. For instance, think about the following attributes:

- Sales reps: In the end, is it *that* important that they update the CRM system versus closing deals and blowing away their quota?
- Marketing: Is implementing a content management system more important than an ability to quantifiably bring in new qualified leads regardless of the source (buying habits do change, after all)?
- Developers: Does the developer need to bang out a lot of lines of code, or do they need to develop bug-free code that end users need and will use (which may mean they need to interact with real users)?
- Managers: What is the most important task? Is it delivering on specific measurements (revenue, etc.) or hiring, leading, and growing a team that will?

Most companies list the dozens of tasks that need to be done instead of the outcomes they want—our BFGs try to distinguish between the two. The long-term benefit of hiring for *outcomes*, not behaviors or tasks, is that your new employee knows exactly how their performance will be measured.

The hiring team can ask questions and look for evidence that these outcomes have been achieved in the past, which can be further verified in reference calls. You can also determine the critical personality traits, values, and characteristics that generally lead to those role-specific outcomes so you can objectively test for those essential traits and values. When you do this, consider soft skills as well as technical skills. Chloe Oddleifson summed this up well when describing Dribbble's approach:

> I think it's super important to have clearly defined parameters for what success looks like within a hire. I would say it's equally [as] important to have well-defined soft skills as it is to have well-defined technical skills. I think that's something that people miss. You can make a great culture hire; someone who's so lovely, friendly, and communicative, but they just miss the hard skills. The flip side is you can have someone who might be an absolute genius, a technical wizard, a super strong engineer, for example, but they're kind of an asshole, and it sucks to work with them. Those are the two extremes you really want to avoid when hiring.

Leverage Job-Focused Formal Assessments to Validate the Interviews

If you've followed a good hiring process, you should have eliminated candidates who are a poor fit for your culture or for the position. You can use assessments to objectively confirm what you already believe to be true about the candidate. But don't assume that assessments and tests will fix a poor hiring process! You should use them as confirmatory evidence only. Assessments can be culture tests, skills, cognitive tests or similar tests such as DiSC Profile, Kolbe Index, and others, but the best case is when they closely resemble the actual job.

Aasha Anam uses AssessFirst for their assessments during recruiting. They assess candidates against the company's three values, with "grit" being the number-one trait they look for. Aasha described to me the rigor they bring to their analysis process. She said, "We were able to build algorithms based on our global top performers." JCW Group uses those algorithms to objectively rank employees using a one to five scale based on their performance and to assess their contributions to the company culture. She said, "It brings a little bit of science and data into what is traditionally quite a difficult thing to do from a subjective viewpoint. . . . The soft skills piece—we're just trying to stamp out the natural unconscious bias that comes whenever you screen for soft skills."

There are many hiring assessment companies out there, so do your homework and find one that objectively measures the traits you are looking for in candidates.

Conduct a Team Interview Based on the Role

By the time you get to the team interview, you should have a sense that the candidate is an excellent cultural fit and that they have the core competencies to do the job. Team interviews ("team" could mean just two people) exist to delve deeper into the candidate's background, desire for the job, and core skills that align with the outcomes you desire for the role.

The team interview can be used in place of the assessment to determine whether the candidate has the core job skills. Behavioral interviews are used to assess the *candidate's potential for growth.*

Be sure to define how your democratic process of hiring will work. At Freestar, every new hire must secure a *unanimous decision*—if anyone says no, they are not hired. This includes the CEO.

We had a team interview process at one of my former companies, but I made the mistake (a few times) of overriding the team's thumbs-down on a candidate because, of course, "I knew in my gut" they were the right hire. If you've been reading along, you know the end of that story—the promising new hire crashed and burned, and Pete had to admit major defeat!

Standardize your interview questions to the greatest extent possible. This will give you control over the data collected by various interviewers. Consistency in how these questions are asked ensures that responses are evaluated uniformly. Such a practice proves particularly valuable when conducting interviews at scale, enhancing the productivity of post-interview debriefs.

Establish key definitions and questions so that everyone works with the same understanding of what the role requires and nobody has to rely on memory for what a good answer looks like.

Use Structured, Behavioral, and Scenario-Based Interviews

Structured, behavioral-based interview questions are designed to understand how candidates have handled specific situations in their past work experiences. These questions can provide valuable insights into their skills, work style, and suitability for a role.

Here are examples of such questions tailored for various roles:

Physical Therapist

- Can you describe a time when you had to adapt a treatment plan because of a patient's changing condition?
- Tell me about a particularly challenging case you managed. What was the situation, and how did you address it?

Software Developer

- Describe a project where you had to learn a new programming language or framework. How did you approach this challenge?
- Can you provide an example of a time when you found a creative solution to a coding problem?

IT Manager

- Share an example of how you led a team through a critical system upgrade or deployment.
- Can you discuss a time when you had to manage a major IT crisis or outage? What steps did you take to resolve the issue?

Financial Analyst

- Tell me about a time when you had to analyze a complex set of financial data. What was your approach, and what conclusions did you draw?
- Describe a situation where you identified a significant financial risk in a project. How did you handle it?

Financial Manager

- Can you discuss a time when you successfully implemented a financial strategy that improved the company's profitability?

- Describe how you have managed a budget cut or financial shortfall in a previous role.

Customer Service Representative

- Describe a situation where you dealt with a difficult customer. How did you handle it, and what was the outcome?
- Tell me about a time when you went above and beyond to solve a customer's problem.

Mechanic

- Tell me about a time when you diagnosed a complex mechanical issue. What was your process, and how did you resolve it?
- Describe a situation where you had to repair a vehicle or machinery under a tight deadline. How did you manage it?

Personal Trainer

- Share an experience where you designed a training program for a client with specific health challenges.
- Can you describe a situation where you had to motivate a client who was struggling with their fitness goals?

When asking these questions, it's essential to listen for specific actions the candidate took and the results of those actions, as this will give you a clearer picture of their capabilities and potential fit for the role. You may be able to go even deeper and more experiential with your process by having the individual demonstrate the role as part of the process. For instance, a candidate for a sales position may be tasked with preparing and delivering a sales presentation, similar to what they would be expected to do in the target position for which they are applying. A candidate for a production assembly position may be tasked with completing portions of the production assembly process that they would be doing on the job.

Scenario-based interviewing, where candidates demonstrate their skills in a role-specific context, can be a highly effective way of assessing their suitability for a position. Here's a list of scenario-based interview processes for various roles:

- Sales position: Prepare and deliver a sales presentation for a product or service relevant to the company's portfolio.
- Production assembly role: Complete specific tasks within the production assembly process under supervised conditions.
- IT technician: Troubleshoot a common IT issue (like a network problem or software glitch) in a simulated environment.
- Software developer: Write a piece of code or debug an existing code snippet related to the company's technology stack.
- Customer service representative: Engage in a role-play scenario handling a customer complaint or query on a call or through written communication.
- Graphic designer: Create a design piece (like a logo or a webpage mockup) using specific design software within a set time frame.
- Project manager: Develop a project plan for a hypothetical project, including timelines, resources, and risk management strategies.
- Financial analyst: Analyze a set of financial data and prepare a report outlining findings, forecasts, and recommendations.
- HR manager: Conduct a mock interview or employee counseling session with a role-playing participant.

- Marketing specialist: Develop a mini-marketing campaign or strategy for a product, including target audience analysis and promotional tactics.

Each scenario should be crafted to mimic real-life job situations as closely as possible, giving the interviewer a clear view of how the candidate would perform in the actual role. It's also important to debrief after the exercise to understand the candidate's thought process and approach.

Check out our Book Resources section at www.scaleupfaster.com/resources to learn more about our AI-based platform to help you upgrade and accelerate your entire hiring process.

Executive Interview

This step was toward the end of the process for every company I spoke with, and the primary purpose was to give the candidate the ability to ask questions about the company and its culture. This was a big test to determine how prepared and engaged the candidate was. Beware the candidate who asks very few questions. All the BFGs that I spoke with said they would reject any candidate who asked generic questions and had clearly done little research on the company.

Reference Checks

When developing a list of questions for checking references for full-time employee candidates, it's crucial to focus on how their past performance and skills align with the outcomes or results they are expected to achieve in the new role.

The following is a structured list of questions that can help you gain insightful information about the candidate's ability to deliver the desired outcomes:

- Understanding of role and responsibilities:
  - Can you describe the candidate's primary responsibilities in their previous role?
  - How did these responsibilities align with your organization's overall goals?
- Achievement of specific outcomes:
  - What were the key outcomes or results the candidate was expected to deliver in their previous role?
  - Can you provide examples of how the candidate successfully achieved these outcomes?
- Problem-solving skills:
  - Can you recall a situation where the candidate faced a significant challenge? How did they address it?
  - What solutions did the candidate propose or implement to overcome obstacles?
- Adaptability and learning:
  - How did the candidate adapt to changes in the workplace, such as shifts in strategic goals or team dynamics?
  - Can you provide an example of how the candidate learned a new skill or concept to perform their duties better?
- Teamwork and collaboration:
  - How effectively did the candidate collaborate with colleagues and other departments?
  - Can you describe a project where the candidate's teamwork contributed significantly to its success?

- Leadership and initiative:
    - Did the candidate take on any leadership roles, formally or informally? How did they perform?
    - Can you provide examples where the candidate demonstrated initiative beyond their regular duties?
- Communication skills:
    - How would you rate the candidate's communication skills, both in writing and orally?
    - Can you give an example of how effective communication played a role in the candidate's success?
- Handling of feedback and improvement:
    - How does the candidate receive and act on feedback?
    - Can you provide an instance where the candidate used constructive criticism to improve their performance?
- Consistency and reliability:
    - Was the candidate consistent in delivering quality work on time?
    - Can you discuss their reliability in meeting deadlines and managing their workload?
- Cultural fit:
    - How did the candidate's work style and attitude align with your organization's culture?
    - Can you provide an example of how the candidate positively contributed to the team or company culture?

- Overall impact:
  - What was the candidate's overall impact on your team and the organization?
  - Would you rehire this candidate if given the opportunity, and why?

Remember, when asking these questions, it's essential to listen for both the content of the answers and the enthusiasm and tone in the reference's responses. Both types of information can provide additional insights into the candidate's performance and potential fit for your organization.

Chapter 3

SUPPORT

Employees who believe that management is concerned about them as a whole person—not just an employee—are more productive, more satisfied, more fulfilled.

—ATTRIBUTED TO ANNE MULCAHY (FORMER CEO OF XEROX)

KEY INSIGHTS

- Figure out how to support employees with meaningful but low-cost benefits in alignment with your culture.
- Make sure the first few weeks for every new employee are mapped out in detail to keep them fully engaged.
- Create a formal mentoring/buddy system to pair every employee with someone who isn't their first-line manager who can serve as a resource.

The BFGs did an outstanding job creating low-cost and no-cost benefits for their employees. Because they were all bootstrapped, they didn't have the money for extensive traditional health benefits, ping pong tables, elaborate offices (although some do now), and above-market compensation. Therefore, they had to get creative in attracting and retaining top talent. As discussed previously, they relied on their cultures to do the heavy lifting but then created very low-cost ways to support every new employee and ensure they were nurtured and fully engaged. What follows are some low-cost ideas you can use in your business to ensure that the employees critical to your success feel nurtured and supported.

Develop Exceptional First Impressions

We intuitively know that first impressions count. The long-term engagement of a new employee starts with the first day the new employee starts and is forged over the course of their first few days and weeks. Did they get an orientation to the company? Did you give them the equipment they need to do their job on the first day? Did you offer any training about the company's organizational structure and their role within it? Did they receive a warm welcome from someone with a vested interest in their success?

I've worked for companies where I did nothing for the first few weeks, and it gave me the impression that the company didn't have their act together. Most employees get some degree of post-purchase dissonance when they join a new company, so you can imagine how confident in your decision you would feel joining an organization where you are so well taken care of from the moment you walk in the door.

The BFGs I spent the most time with nailed this process. For instance, Freestar maps out the first two weeks for every new hire, hour by hour. This is shared with every new employee when they start so that they know what is expected of them. Farmgirl Flowers has an employee experience manager who ensures every employee is fully engaged and cared for. The workload for new employees is light for the first two weeks. They have a lot of conference calls with managers to make connections, get to know people, and ease into the job. As Lindsey Whalen Draska said, this helps them "'live into the organization' and sets them up for success in their remote and working environment." She shared more details of their process with me:

> The one thing that has been a significant deal maker is when we implemented this thirty/sixty/ninety day plan when the hiring manager asks us to post a role. They have to have the job description polished and ready to go, and they also have to come up with their thirty/sixty/ninety-day plan. That helps in the interview process because we can speak to specifically what they will experience in the first thirty days. It's a really great way to set people up for success.

JCW Group has a "vertical buddy system," so everybody in the company has a person assigned to them who's not in their team and more senior than them to help with their career goals, issues they're struggling with, or just general advice. The buddy is intentionally not in their reporting vertical but is someone they might work with. Everybody is assigned a buddy when they join the business, regardless of their level and function. Kate Turner, partner and HR director for Search Capital, said the buddy system helps their employees with questions like these: "I've got this happening with a client. Have you ever had this? How did you resolve it?" She said the power of this system is that they have "a buddy they can go to with anything they can't resolve themselves or through their immediate supervisor."[1]

In the first week on the job, managers sit down with their new hires and ask them about their favorite projects they've done, the moments when they've felt most energized at work, the times when they've found themselves totally immersed in a state of flow, and the passions they have outside their jobs. Armed with that knowledge, managers can build engaging roles from the start.

Getting the first few days, weeks, and months right will go a long way toward higher employee engagement and productivity and longer retention. If you let them figure it out themselves for a few weeks, you'll end up watching that person leave your company when you least expect it, and you'll have wasted the time and expense you put into hiring them.

Institutionalize Employee Recognition

Ensuring that you are getting the best performance out of each member is *really* inexpensive. You do it by showing your team members that you care about them and appreciate their efforts! Leaders of companies that grow faster create a culture of recognition, which helps them have engaged teams that produce better results.

According to research by OC Tanner, a staggering 79 percent of employees who voluntarily leave their jobs cite a lack of appreciation as a significant factor in their decision. An astonishing 65 percent of Americans reported not receiving recognition over the past year. And based on extensive research by GoLEAD, 82 percent of employees feel their bosses don't give them enough credit for their efforts. A remarkable 60 percent of those surveyed said that recognition motivates them more than getting extra money.[2]

When leaders give their team members the recognition they deserve, express appreciation genuinely, and acknowledge everyone's unique qualities, they can achieve better results. At the same time, they boost the spirits of everyone involved, including themselves, creating a positive atmosphere that spreads throughout the organization.

This includes using trust and transparency as recognition. Kurt

Donnell, the president and CEO at Freestar, shares the company's key performance indicators (KPIs) because he believes you should treat people like adults.[3] This engenders trust in the organization, which I saw firsthand throughout my interactions with the Freestar team. Kurt understands that the employees may share this information with competitors, but he firmly believes that if you hire great people, you need to trust them and give them the information they need to help the company be successful.

Our BFGs identified the simple and powerful act of giving constant, job-related recognition (which is rarely executed well) as a vital tool for retention and high performance. The BFG leaders effectively set specific goals and behavioral expectations that they knew would lead to good results and then sincerely recognized those behaviors as they witnessed them! They made recognition meaningful, which motivated the employees to achieve the desired results.

By including recognition in their daily routines, the BFG leaders made regular feedback (positive and negative) a natural part of how they lead. Surprisingly, this small investment in time seemed to boost even the leaders' performance because their team members became more motivated to help them. Christy Rosensteel, general counsel and chief people officer for Freestar, told me about their approach:

> Every week, anyone can [nominate] someone for a "taking care of business" award, and they're recognized in our weekly newsletter and also get a $50 gift card. Reading through them warms your heart to see. Oh my gosh, this person did this . . . or they went out of their way—they didn't know this, but they took on this project. We really want people to shout out other folks on their team or other teams doing great things. . . . They get their photo and the write-up in the weekly newsletter for that.

Create a Competitive, Performance-Based Compensation and Benefits Package

None of the BFGs I interviewed compensated their employees at the high end of the market for their roles. Most paid their employees around the average compensation for their industry, geography, and roles. A few even admitted that they paid below the average, then let their cultures attract the right kind of people who weren't simply seeking the highest wages. Some admitted that this got tougher as they grew larger and expanded into new markets, so they constantly reevaluated their compensation levels. Most BFGs that wanted to pay higher wages did so through incentive-based/variable compensation. They wanted to attract high performers, so they paid higher than their market based on exceptional performance.

One method of variable compensation that I used in my last company was to align the performance-based compensation of our employees to the direct impact they had on the satisfaction and loyalty of our customers. I had a consulting firm, and we used the Net Promoter Score (NPS) survey to measure the health of our customer relationships; it was a precise measure of their level of loyalty. Because virtually every employee had some impact on our relationships with our customers, from the consultants on the ground to our billing department to the receptionist who answered the phone, we tied everyone's compensation to both the overall NPS score of the company and the score for the individual consultant.

When we asked our customers, on a scale of one to ten, "How likely they would be to recommend EntryPoint (the name of my previous firm) to a friend or colleague," we included a question that asked the same about the individual consultant(s) working on their project. In other words, we'd ask, on a scale of one to ten, how likely they would be to refer the specific consultant to a friend or colleague.

We then created a variable compensation matrix that showed how much variable compensation (the bonus percentage of their salary) they would get based on the intersection of the overall and individual scores. If the customer loved the company but didn't like the consultant, they were paid less or none of their bonus. If they loved the consultant but had issues with the company, they were paid some of their bonus but not all.

The effect of this compensation scheme made sure that every employee was focused not only on their individual performance but on the company's overall reputation as well. Typically, employees hear gripes from customers, but they never pass along the information to the proper department to fix until it's too late. This plan ensured that any customer issue that arose was addressed immediately because the employee who heard the complaint knew their compensation was partially based on the company score. We structured the plan such that if the customer was a promoter for the company *and* the individual, the employee overachieved their bonus percentage.

The variable compensation matrix is shown in Table 3.1 (the percentages in the table reflect the percent of their salary they receive as a bonus).

Table 3.1. Variable compensation matrix

		Individual consultant NPS		
		9.0–10	6.0–8.9	0–5.9
Practice/company NPS	9.0–10	15%	5%	0%
	6.0–8.9	10%	3%	0%
	0–5.9	5%	0%	0%

Check out our Book Resources section at www.scaleupfaster.com/resources for a template of our NPS variable compensation plan you can use in your company.

On the benefits side of the house, most BFGs were very cost efficient in assembling a bucket of benefits that employees found beneficial and complementary to their compensation. Benefits such as work-from-anywhere plans and money for essential home office equipment ensured the employee was as productive as possible. Kyle Mitnick shared Advertise Purple's process with me:

> We allocate 5 percent of annual revenue toward employee wellness. That includes our actual insurance plans and [other traditional benefits]. A significant amount of that expense is for individual team events weekly per department; we do department-wide events, companywide events, for instance, taco trucks, pizza trucks, and stuff around town. We have a President's Club out of the country with top producers once a year. We invest in the health and wellness of the employees to make sure they're gelled together because they're connected at the hip when they're here at work.[4]

JCW Group conducts a Happiness Survey that includes personal and professional considerations to ensure that they care for as many of their employees' needs as possible. It's very simple and inexpensive and gives them insights about potential culture-building benefits that keep their employees engaged and productive.

It takes virtually no effort or expense to figure out what level of compensation and benefits will motivate your employees, improve their productivity, and ensure their long-term success—just ask them! Employees rarely leave purely because of compensation issues. If you ensure that you are paying them fairly and incentivizing exceptional performance and providing the sort of benefits that fit your culture, you can hire and support top-performing teams like our BFGs.

Managers Will Make or Break Your Organization

People join companies. They leave managers.
—VERNE HARNISH, *Scaling Up*

In a study involving 7,272 U.S. adults, the survey company Gallup found that 50 percent of employees left their jobs at some point to escape an ineffective manager and enhance their overall quality of life.[5] This conclusion, drawn from decades of Gallup's research and interviews with twenty-five million employees, underscores the importance of selecting the right managers. Gallup CEO Jim Clifton asserts that selecting a manager is the most critical decision in one's company.[6] When the wrong person assumes a managerial position, no amount of compensation or benefits can rectify the resulting damage.

Nevertheless, many companies continue to falter, spending substantial resources on various initiatives while neglecting the fundamental aspect of managerial selection. Having a subpar manager is a double blow because employees suffer during work hours, and this misery follows them home, magnifying the stress and hurting their overall well-being. But just as a poor manager can tarnish a promising job, an exceptional manager can elevate an already positive work experience.

The support I talk about in this section comes from both the company and, even more so, the immediate manager. Effectively managing people is often one of the most challenging aspects of sustaining a growing company, so you should dedicate a lot of attention to nurturing and developing competent managers. DLP Capital is keenly aware of this, and their recruiting and development focus is on hiring future leaders. They understand how critical a manager is to the success of each employee and team, so their support and developmental processes are focused on growing great leaders. This was the case for many of our BFGs. Chloe Oddleifson told me about Dribbble's approach:

> Something we are very particular about is training our managers. [We want] leadership that's aligned on how to lead their teams, like making sure that there's a leadership philosophy on what's important to us when we're coaching our people and when we're working to get results from people. We have a very clear definition of what a manager does at Dribbble, why we have managers and what the expectations are of managers. Because I think that's where good performance management starts, right?

As Chloe states, good performance management starts with good management. By effectively hiring and upskilling good managers, you'll go a long way toward an effective high-performance culture. Most companies simply promote good individual performers to management positions. This stems from individual performers who want to be, and think they can be, good managers, and from companies who believe the best way to reward good performance is to promote people into management positions. But the skills and competencies required to be an exceptional individual contributor are very different from those needed to be an effective manager. I can't emphasize this enough. If I could do a Tom Cruise impression and jump on a couch and shout this statement, I would.

I experienced this in my corporate career several times. I ended up working for managers who were promoted because they had great success as individual contributors—but they were horrible managers and I quit my jobs because of it. (Okay, I know what you're thinking: Pete, you're an entrepreneur, and you can't work for someone else anyway. Well, you're right. Guilty as charged.)

Before you give someone that promotion, evaluate their core competencies against someone you would hire from the outside. If they have what it takes but just need some training, great, go for it. But many times, by objectively evaluating their fundamental talents, you'll realize that they're not cut out to be a manager. If this is the case, create a career path that allows them to grow and flourish but that doesn't involve having to manage people.

Focus Your Performance Management on Catching Behaviors as They Happen

Many of our BFGs dislike the traditional performance review structure. They've replaced it with ongoing coaching and on-the-spot feedback that gives employees the information they need to drive their own performance improvements. For example, Kate Turner explained that an individual's performance is monitored through Search Capital's Performance and Development Support Plan. Their focus is on the positive developmental aspects of an individual's performance instead of a backward-looking focus on what they did or didn't do.

This was also the case for Odyssey Engineering Group. Ellen Hughes told us that they don't do performance reviews; they set goals for specific areas of professional improvement. Mentoring reinforces and supports this because they ask their top performers to help support and teach others. Ellen explained the process in more detail:

> They're not even like reviews because they're done every six months and are more like goal settings. You do a goal setting around March, and then we review it somewhere in the summer. Managers focus on how you are doing on your goals and occasionally redirect people, but we think you shouldn't be waiting six months to tell someone that their engineering work is not on par. We also do other little things like kudos that anyone can send. Any manager can come to me

> and get a kudo, and I give them a blank card and a $10 gift card to Starbucks or something. And they write it out, and it's immediate.

I previously worked for very large companies like IBM and SAP that had very robust performance management processes, and I was struck by how sophisticated many of the BFG's performance management systems were for the size and maturity of their companies—without having formal performance management processes. That's a confusing statement, I know. What I mean is that their performance management plan focused heavily on coaching, not performance management, and they created processes and programs to foster the day-to-day collaboration that really improves behaviors and skills. They tried different methods to align the company's goals with the growth and performance of the individual. Some methods worked, and some failed miserably, like at Advertise Purple.

Advertise Purple has a sales-heavy culture. The leadership team decided to institute a metrics-based performance management system called Global Scores, where they ranked employees publicly on a leaderboard system. Jonathan Moisan told me how they adapted their approach based on feedback from their staff members:

> The feedback we got was, well, you're micromanaging us. Each person works differently, and some clients are easier than others. I think it was a combination of being compared to other people and we didn't do it like this before. I could see myself being an entry-level employee and wanting to explain that I'm at the bottom of the list because of this and that—so it's not fair. It just created a door for too many nuances and too many what-ifs. We were seeing numbers without the context behind it.

> And people were being judged on those numbers and they felt it wasn't fair.

The point here is that sometimes you don't know what will work. So experiment and find a way to assess and monitor performance that creates a positive environment and not a punitive one. Too many performance management programs focus on historical performance and not forward progress. It's like the old saying, you can't drive a car by looking in the rearview mirror.

To objectively measure the overall employee health of the company, many of our BFGs used an Employee Net Promoter Score (eNPS) survey every few months. I won't get into the details of NPS in this book, but it's a methodology developed initially for measuring customer loyalty. Companies began using the same approach to measure employee loyalty, and the eNPS was born. Because the NPS score is a forward-looking index, the BFGs were able to address any emerging issues in advance, which resulted in all of them having excellent employee retention numbers with virtually no significant employee layoffs.

Here's my pro tip for you: Measure managers on successes of their individual team members and move them from being a manager to being a coach. For instance, instead of measuring a sales manager on whether she makes her revenue number, measure her on the percentage of quota attainment for each team member she's responsible for. Assuming each team member achieves their quota, the manager would make her overall revenue goal. Measuring the manager on each team member's attainment will completely change the interactions between the manager and their subordinate.

Chapter 4

GROW

The thing that motivates and engages beyond money or praise is learning. It's what turns our organizations into talent magnets.

—WHITNEY JOHNSON, *BUILD AN A-TEAM*

KEY INSIGHTS

- If you don't invest in developing your employees, they will leave sooner than you want.
- You can create exceptional learning and development programs inexpensively by being creative and using affordable resources.

If You Don't Invest in Your Employees, They Will Leave

Employees who say they use their strengths every day are 8% more productive and 15% less likely to quit their jobs.

—STEVE CRABTREE, "Strengths-Based Cultures Are Vital to the Future of Work"

If people are your most important asset, do you invest in them the way you would any asset you want to appreciate?

Let's think about this for a moment.

You hire a capable person, and you invest in training them. The fear is if you train them, they will leave or ask for more money. Yet, if you invested in your home, business, or anything that improves your assets, you would expect it to increase in value! Why shouldn't it be the same with your employees? (You did say they were your greatest asset, right?)

If you invest in improving their skills, they should also appreciate and increase in value. But like any underappreciated asset, if someone else realizes the value differential, they will take advantage of it and hire your employees away.

What does "grow" mean in the context of people? And if you do invest in growing your people, how do you keep them from leaving?

The Facebook people analytics team recently crunched data to predict which new employees would stay or leave within six months. Through this research, they learned some interesting facts about those who remained. The people who stayed found their work enjoyable 31 percent more often, used their strengths 33 percent more often, and expressed 37 percent more confidence that they were gaining the skills and experiences they needed to develop their careers. This demonstrates the need to ensure employees utilize their skills to the fullest and develop, learn, and grow.[1]

Bobby Frazitta explained to me how RIVA Solutions implements this process for their entire staff:

> Every time we do a quarterly review, we require all the managers to document not just the good, the bad, and whatever, not just what they are doing well in their day-to-day job, but what are they doing around their career development. We're putting together, by level, required training that we want people to do, and it's basically to enhance their soft skills like empathy, emotional intelligence, and things that build some competencies outside of their day-to-day work.

To reinforce this point, when I looked at the leadership teams of the BFGs I interviewed, they were generally earlier in their careers. They were put into positions above their experience levels, meaning they experienced significant personal and professional growth.

This didn't always work out perfectly, as I heard a few stories from some of the BFGs who had to part with loyal team members as they hit certain growth thresholds and had to up-skill the organization. But this hire-and-grow-talent philosophy mirrored the founders' journeys—most were first-time founders and had raised their skills substantially since founding their companies.

The number two reason people leave is that they don't see growth opportunities. When I sold my consulting firm to KPMG, it was partly because I felt we didn't have enough development headroom for the team to grow and develop. KPMG had outstanding professional development programs, and I knew the team could thrive there and go further and faster.

A common objection to spending time and money on training is that "if I train them, they'll just use that training and go to a competitor!" This is a legitimate risk, but I am confident, and the statistics prove it, that if you are *not* developing your people, then the chances are greater than 50 percent that they will leave your company anyway. Even if they don't quit, their level of engagement (and consequently, their productivity) will be low, and you will not be leveraging the greatest source of long-term profitability you have!

Another common objection is that if you train them, they'll ask for more money. This is another genuine risk, but it's your job as the leader to ensure that your people are paid a fair wage. If they are not professionally growing at your company, the flight risk is high, just like it is if you are not paying them market-rate wages.

With the advent of remote work, your competitors (which might have been other local companies in the past) could come from anywhere. If your employees' skills improve and their ability to perform a bigger job at a higher level or at a higher productivity rate improves, then they should earn more money!

What is the point of all of this?

If your employees are not learning and growing in some way, they will likely become less engaged and less productive, and they are more likely to leave.

The overall goal is to be a leader in productivity, which can be measured in many different ways but is frequently measured as revenue or profit per employee.

DLP Capital's singular focus is to be the most productive company in the world. According to their CEO, Don Wenner:

> When you focus on productivity as a metric, it becomes a bit of a forcing function to ensure that you get the maximum productivity out of everyone. This journey can be undertaken on a top-down basis. Getting your team to work harder, more productively, or longer hours is a recipe for disaster, and you'll quickly find that you have a disengaged and unproductive team ready to head to the exits.

Instead, productivity improvement comes primarily from increasing the skills and knowledge of your team through upskilling, either through hiring new people or training your current team. Many types of training, including on-the-job and formal training, can be offered. Each role and each person will have different needs, but you must develop an individual plan directly with each person. Jonathan Moisan of Advertise Purple talked about this when I interviewed him:

> Anytime someone comes to us with, "Can you pay for this SEO class that I want to take?" or "I want to get my Google Analytics certification," we will support, pay, and sponsor almost anything that anyone comes to us with, and a lot of people take advantage of that. We buy books for entire departments and say, let's read these and have a conversation about them. That care goes a long way. They see that we don't *have* to do these things, but we do. It's helping with retention and helping our employees. Why wouldn't we make a small investment to pay for that?

Provide Employees with a Variety of Trainings

Our BFGs were experts at creating learning and development opportunities in cost-effective ways. All the teams I interviewed were consistent in the ways they were thoughtful about creating programs to allow their employees to learn and grow. Perhaps because they were learning organizations from the beginning, this just came naturally to them. What follows are the various areas for which you should offer training.

WORK SKILLS TRAINING

Have your team members put together a list of the fundamental skills that, if mastered, would lead to exceptional performance and improved job satisfaction. Have them generate ideas for how to best enhance an individual's work skills.

LIFE SKILLS TRAINING

Depending on the level(s) of employees you hire into your organization, you may need to offer life skills training. This ranges from enhanced academic classes in math and English to personal financial management. At JCW Group, they provide external training in "first aid" for mental health concerns so that colleagues can identify potential mental health issues in their teammates. Farmgirl Flowers provides practicum training, such as powerful listening. Both companies want to ensure that each one of their employees brings their whole self to the workplace, and they are committed to providing the support and training necessary to ensure this.

PROFESSIONAL TRAINING (LEADERSHIP)

Very few people are born with exceptional leadership skills, and virtually every critical skill a successful leader would need can be taught. Many companies make the mistake of moving high-performing individual contributors into leadership positions with zero training and assume they'll be as productive as they were in the individual contributor role. Not everyone is cut out to be a great manager or leader, so assessing the core capabilities for serving in this function is essential before handing out that promotion.

CROSS-FUNCTIONAL TRAINING

Providing employees with a broader set of skills allows you to have a contingency plan if you lose a key team member and allows team members to appreciate their colleagues better. But not all roles can be cross trained effectively. You probably don't want to cross-train your administrative staff at the hospital to be brain surgeons. Still, there are definitely ways to get your brain surgeons to spend a day working the front lines to understand and appreciate others' functions. This is akin to having developers listen in on customer support calls or salespeople and the CEO spending a day on support calls so that everyone appreciates the customer's needs.

Create Exceptional Learning and Development Programs Inexpensively

Like compensation and benefits, our BFGs excelled at creating robust and comprehensive learning and development programs that cost little to no money. Additionally, the cost of training employees has decreased dramatically in the past five years, and robust training catalogs are available from Udemy and Coursera and leadership training from the Growth Institute.

Our BFGs came up with numerous inexpensive ways to upskill their teams, which gave them a substantially higher return on investment (ROI) (i.e., saving money) on training, including the following programs. Shamelessly steal these ideas and implement your comprehensive learning and development program immediately—whether you have two employees or two hundred.

MENTORING AND COACHING

This is the most cost-effective way to help employees grow and provides multiple benefits, from advanced learning to additional support. Many people learn when they teach so even the mentors get value out of the relationship because they need to clarify and crystalize their thinking as they coach and mentor others.

BOOK GROUPS

Book groups are an excellent and inexpensive way to enhance learning (assuming your employees are into reading) and create community. I was surprised to learn that most of the BFGs had formal book groups, ranging from special topic groups (female leadership and active listening) to more weighty business topics. The groups were all voluntary to join and open to everyone. They were actively promoted and well-received. In many cases, it gave newer and lower-level employees direct and unfiltered access to executives in the BFG companies. In some of our BFGs, the employees take turns leading or facilitating the book clubs, and some BFGs provide off-site workshops on various topics like storytelling, values, or leadership. Sometimes the CEO even leads those workshops!

E-LEARNING COURSES

The cost of offering online training/e-learning has decreased significantly in the past five years. There are robust training catalogs for every role in every industry platform from organizations such as Udemy, Coursera, LinkedIn, and the Growth Institute, to name a few. Many of these platforms can create individual learning curricula for roles, departments, and individuals, so it takes minimal effort and cost to create individualized development programs for each employee.

STANDARD OPERATING PROCEDURES

Some of our BFGs used the process of documenting operational processes to train new and existing employees. Plenty of tools help do this, from VidGuide, Trainual, Process Street, Connecteam, Rippling (and a lot more). Ideally, the standard operating procedures (SOPs) that are created are video-rich and checklist-oriented. Having employees create SOPs not only is a learning opportunity but also allows an individual group to actively question workflows and eliminate and automate tasks, which puts your team in control of their work, leading to a more productive (and lower stress) workforce. This provides enormous benefits by standardizing and documenting operational processes and identifying areas for automating or eliminating mundane tasks.

Identify the depth and breadth of skills needed to keep everyone learning and growing, then develop multiple avenues to accomplish this like the ones above. Your ability to grow and scale faster will be largely dependent on how fast you learn and grow as an organization. There is no perfect learning and development program, so create one that fits your culture and get started today. Mentoring, lunch and learns, book clubs, and SOPs can be executed with zero dollars, so there is no excuse not to implement them.

Check out our Book Resources section at www.scaleupfaster.com/resources for our *Definitive Guide to Standard Operating Procedures* ebook.

Chapter 5

RELEASE

The moment you feel the need to tightly manage someone, you've made a hiring mistake. The best people don't need to be managed. Guided, taught, led—yes. But not tightly managed.

—JIM COLLINS, *GOOD TO GREAT*

KEY INSIGHTS

- Stop micromanaging if you want to grow faster.
- Implement systems and processes slightly in advance of your size and complexity.
- Identify and socialize KPIs that everyone can influence.
- Become expert at effective delegation.
- Manage outcomes, not processes.

Stop Micromanaging If You Want to Grow Faster

When I talk about "release" in this chapter, I am talking about the CEO and leadership teams letting go, not micromanaging, and putting systems and processes in place so the company can grow and scale faster. This is a common problem of young, growing companies where the founder/owner/CEO can't let go of critical functions, and it stifles the growth of the company.

To uncover this issue, I asked the CEOs in our interviews how many hours they worked, how many vacations they took, and for how long. I also asked them whether they had personal or executive assistants. I'm sure they thought these were strange questions, but there was a method to my madness. With these questions and subsequent ones with their leadership teams, I wanted to discover whether they had built self-managing teams or had killed themselves micromanaging and trying to control everything. I assumed they had done an effective job of creating self-managing organizations because it's virtually impossible to scale at the rate of growth our BFGs did by trying to do everything themselves—but I wanted to find out for sure.

To begin with, I discovered that the BFGs were pretty normal when it came to the hours they worked and the amount of free time they took. All of them stated that they worked an average forty-eight to fifty hours per week and took one or two vacations per year of at least one week in length. They all admitted to working while on vacation, but most said it was just to check in. Very few of them, even those CEOs running companies with more than $100 million in annual revenue, had executive assistants, and I concluded that this was just part of their lean bootstrapped ideology (I didn't ask why they did or didn't employ them).

I then asked their leadership teams a series of questions to uncover the level of micromanagement inside the organization. I heard a few murmurs about some micromanagement but when I dug in, it seemed to only happen when the CEO felt that a functional leader or department was not performing.

You know your employees want autonomy. They want opportunities for growth and to build things. You want to attract the people who join your firm because they know they'll be able to be creative and generate results without having to fight a micromanager or bureaucracy.

The bottom-line is this (I know it's probably common sense): If you want to grow faster, you have to hire a competent leadership team that complements your culture and agrees on the North Star metrics you want to track. And then you have to let them do their thing.

Identify and Socialize Key Performance Indicators That Everyone Can Influence

Share KPI's and treat people like adults. They may share with competitors, but if you hire and trust them, it will work.

—**KURT DONNELL, Freestar**

Just like a driver needs to know their speed, fuel level, and engine performance to win a race, a company needs KPIs to measure how well they're doing and where they can improve. But the magic happens when the KPIs are shared and understood by everyone in the company. This is like having every member of the racing team, from the driver to the engineers, knowing exactly what's needed to win. When everyone understands what those key measures are—like customer satisfaction scores (many of the BFGs used NPS), sales targets, or product quality—they can see how their daily work makes a real difference. This creates a powerful sense of team spirit and purpose.

But here's the key: These KPIs need to be ones that everyone can have an impact on in some way. It's like giving each team member a part of the car to look after. If only the driver knows the plan and the rest of the team is in the dark, the race can't be won. When everyone knows what's important, from the person answering phones to the one closing deals, they can all work toward common goals.

When teams are united and working toward clear, shared goals, the company can move faster. This unity not only speeds up growth but also makes the journey more enjoyable and fulfilling for everyone involved. Identifying and socializing KPIs that everyone can affect isn't just a good business practice; it's a growth accelerator. It turns a group of individuals into a unified team, all pulling in the same direction toward success. Our BFGs universally did a good job of socializing the objectives and making sure that each person knew how their daily work affected the objectives of the company.

Become an Expert Delegator

Entrepreneurs start companies and leverage their unique skills to grow the business. As they achieve success, many founders fall into the same trap, where they hold on to too many responsibilities and struggle to delegate tasks effectively. I found that mastering the art and science of delegation is a prerequisite to growing faster and to building a company that can thrive beyond the founder/owner.

In addition, effective delegation away from the founder/CEO has a direct impact on the valuation of the company. If the owner ever wants a successful exit, they'll need to demonstrate that the business can run without them.

I experienced this personally when I sold my third company to KPMG. We had completed due diligence, finished redlining the Asset Purchase Agreement, and were ready to close. But the process slowed to almost a dead stop. When I inquired why the deal seemed to stall, I was directed to meet with the vice chair, who was the ultimate decision-maker. When I met with him, he voiced his concern that I wasn't part of the deal (I wasn't staying on after the purchase), and that they generally didn't acquire companies where the business owner/CEO didn't stay on for a period of time. Fortunately, in anticipation of selling, I had spent a year transitioning all the critical business functions to my leadership team so I could focus solely on strategic activities. If I hadn't done that proactively, I wouldn't have sold the business or would have been tied into long earnouts or staying on for a number of years. Most importantly, once I backed off and gave the reins to the team, we grew faster! Many founders don't realize that through their well-meaning actions, they stifle the growth of their business.

Here is a framework for actionable steps an owner can take to increase their company's value and delegate tasks in ways that will help their business operate without their everyday involvement. The four degrees of delegation is a simple formula to master the art of delegation that will help you solve operational issues and, more importantly, help you scale faster and drive up the value of your company.

THE FIRST DEGREE OF DELEGATION: FOLLOW MY LEAD

The first degree of delegation is when you trust an employee to follow your SOPs, and they must follow your process. They are not being given any decision-making authority, and you're not open to accommodating many variables. This kind of delegation is suitable for common tasks where you're clear on what you want done and how you want someone to do it.

THE SECOND DEGREE OF DELEGATION: RESEARCH AND REPORT

The second degree of delegation involves giving an employee a broader scope of responsibility and asking them to come up with solutions for completing a project or task, but the decision about which course of action to take remains with you. This kind of delegation is ideal when you don't have the answer to a specific problem, and you'd like possible solutions. These are usually important decisions that could have a negative impact, and therefore you want to stay involved and make the final decision.

THE THIRD DEGREE OF DELEGATION: DO IT AND REPORT

The third degree of delegation involves giving the employee decision-making authority because you trust them to make a decision. This level of delegation also requires that they inform you of those decisions so you can course correct if needed. This trust in your employee(s) starts to get them thinking like an owner. Although very few of the BFGs had employee stock option plans, everyone I spoke with acted like owners in large part because of the level of responsibility given to their teams.

THE FOURTH DEGREE OF DELEGATION: JUST DO IT

This level of delegation is used when you trust an employee to completely remove something from your plate. It is best used when you have provided an employee with an SOP for completing a task and the impacts of a bad decision are relatively manageable. It can also be appropriate to use the fourth degree of delegation if a task is something you know little about and would be better handled by someone who is more knowledgeable.

In addition to defining the degree of delegation, you'll also want to consider whether a time or monetary budget is required. For example, at the Ritz-Carlton hotel chain, each employee, regardless of level, is given a $2,000 budget to fix a guest's problem. Ritz-Carlton is using the fourth degree of delegation (do it) and empowering staff at all levels to make a guest's problem go away, provided it can be done for less than $2,000. Each employee at Ritz-Carlton knows they have the decision-making authority to act up to a specific spending threshold. For example, if a bellhop damages a piece of luggage, they know they can—and are expected to—replace the piece of luggage, provided they can do so for less than $2,000.

Check out our Book Resources section at www.scaleupfaster.com/resources for our *4 Degrees of Delegation* ebook. Delegating can be hard for business owners (which I heard from most of our BFGs). Our Delegator Tool will help you hone your delegation skills by taking you through a framework for delegating activities effectively.

Manage Outcomes, Not Processes

Our BFGs generally did a very good job of leading by focusing on outcomes or goals they wanted to achieve. With a few exceptions, they weren't overly prescriptive in how they went about aligning their teams to achieve their objectives, but most had a cadence of monthly and quarterly check-ins and annual business planning. Once they established the objectives, they let their teams figure out how to get there. They did a good job getting their teams to focus on the outcomes and giving them the freedom to figure out the best way to reach the goal. This approach encouraged the teams to be creative and solve problems, making them feel more important and involved in the project. Being flexible led to more efficient methods and even better outcomes, especially as each company grew through the various stages of operational maturity, which created new ways of working in each phase.

PART II

Customers

activate →
acquire →
nurture →
co-innovate

Most businesses get zero channels to work: poor sales rather than bad product is the most common cause of failure. If you can get just one distribution channel to work, you have a great business. If you try for several but don't nail one, you're finished.

—**PETER THIEL, *ZERO TO ONE***

Your Stall at the Market

Let's start this part with an analogy.

Imagine you're selling your products or services at a bustling street market. Each stall is different, selling unique items, but you all share one goal: to attract (and keep) new customers. A stream of prospective customers walks up and down the aisles, glancing at each stall, sometimes stopping to look a little closer but most of the time just walking by with barely a glance. And even though you believe your product or service is unique and different from the other stalls, your prospective customers view your stall as pretty much the same as the others. Your pricing is similar (neither premium nor lowest price), and you want to ensure that you get the lion's share of the new business from this constant stream of customers.

What do you do?

This is the fundamental question of any business that seeks to grow faster, which I explore in this part. It's never been more challenging to stand out in the crowd and acquire new customers consistently and cost-effectively. I will examine how the BFGs grow faster by consistently acquiring new customers more profitably than their competitors.

There are now countless competitors in every industry and so much marketing noise that prospects ignore most pitches. Companies have an endless supply of ways to suck up their customers' money in the pursuit of growth, and plenty of experts, gurus, and advisors are ready to sell the "best method" to those companies.

To make matters even more challenging, in comes generative artificial intelligence (AI) apps, such as ChatGPT, which will profoundly change how we discover new products and services!

In this part, I'll explore each phase of the customer lifecycle, including how our BFGs attract (marketing), acquire (sales), and nurture (service) new customers profitably enough to allow them to grow faster than their competitors while bootstrapping their growth.

You'll be surprised by what I discovered!

A Little Primer

Your company is like one of these stalls in our example above. The challenge is finding the right way to draw people to your stall and away from the other competitive stalls and keep them coming back.

But which strategy (channel) should you choose?

To set the stage, I want to provide a few definitions.

Channels are avenues to reach your customers. Each channel comprises various tactics that require specific skills and assets to take advantage of the channel.

Tactics includes activities such as sending cold emails, chat, InMail, and tradeshow sponsorships.

Generally, most customer acquisition (marketing) strategies can be categorized into six channels:

1. *SEO and inbound:* This is about catching people who are actively searching for what you offer.
2. *Paid advertising:* Simply put, it's buying ads on any medium—web, TV, radio, and so on.
3. *Organic social and influencers:* Engaging an audience with content.
4. *Outbound direct sales:* Directly reaching out to potential customers.
5. *Viral or product-led:* Where your customers help bring in more customers.
6. *Partners or resellers:* Others sell your product as part of their business.

Deciding which channel suits your business isn't about finding one that works—they all do. (Frustrating, I know—c'mon, Pete—give me the answer!) It's about figuring out which one your team can excel in. But each channel has its own set of challenges, particularly at scale. For example, ponder these data points:

- In SEO, Backlinko studied four million search results and found that the top three results get 54.4 percent of all clicks, and less than 1 percent of people clicked on the second page of results.[1] Can you effectively reach your category's first page on Google or Bing?
- Paid ads are a competitive auction in which the highest bidder wins. Are you willing to spend the most to get in front of your best prospects?
- Despite its effectiveness, the top influencers (think of the Kardashians) dominate organic social media. Are you ready to record, post, and tweet videos of meaningful (or at least click-worthy) content several times daily?
- With direct sales, prospects get inundated with sales pitches and generally tune them out. Are you prepared to hire a highly paid sales force to chase them?

So how do you choose the right channel for your business? First, you must consider these three factors:

1. Does the chosen acquisition channel align with your business structure and culture?
2. Does it match your team's (internal or external) skills and abilities?
3. Do you know how much money you can spend to acquire each new customer?

Before I explore what our BFGs do exceptionally well, here are some guiding questions as you consider whether each channel can help you grow your business faster:

- SEO and inbound: Is your target market searching online for solutions you offer? Can you produce great content and rank high in searches?

- Paid advertising: Can your product capture attention quickly? Do you have strong copywriting and design skills? Can you afford the cost?
- Organic social and influencers: Do your customers follow influencers? Is your product visually appealing or does it have a great story? Can you work with top influencers?
- Outbound direct sales: Is your product complex or high-priced? Can you cover your costs with your sales team? Do you have strong sales and lead-gen skills?
- Viral or product-led: Does using your product naturally encourage customers to invite others?
- Partners or resellers: Does your product complement another product or service?

The key is to pick the best one for your business and focus on mastering it. It takes time and continuous experimentation to master a channel. Growing your company faster isn't about being everywhere at once. It's about finding where you fit best, focusing your efforts, and continuously refining your approach. Like the stalls in the market, the secret is understanding your space and making the most of it.

With a few definitions and key learnings out of the way, I dig into how these fantastic companies grew their sales faster than their competitors. I go deeper into the lessons learned across all our BFGs, covering all the steps of the customer lifecycle from acquisition to retention, and supplement that information with specific examples of what I believe are exceptional practices by our BFGs in each phase of growth.

Now, let's find out what makes our BFGs successful at growing faster on shoestring budgets.

Chapter 6

ACTIVATE (MARKETING)

KEY INSIGHTS

- Forget what you've learned about marketing; it's your job to create and capture the demand by activating customers' interests.
- Pick one growth lever to master.
- Create and foster your community.
- Double down on what makes you unique—even if it's weird and counterintuitive.

According to the U.S. Small Business Administration, high-growth organizations that aim to grow by 30 percent yearly require 10 to 25 percent of annual revenue budgeted for sales and marketing. Of that percentage, marketing should consume about one-third of that budget or 7 to 8 percent of revenue. Of that amount, they advise that 40 percent go toward headcount and 60 percent toward campaign spending.[1] Paradoxically, the marketing budgets and teams at the companies I interviewed were very light in terms of people and dollars.

Our BFGs seem to do more with less. The average spending on marketing and lead generation was around 2.5 percent of yearly revenue, and the marketing leaders within these companies were generally brought on later in the company's lifecycle.

What our BFGs did consistently well was test, measure, and refine their customer acquisition strategies. CAC was the most mentioned important measurement, along with ROAS for the companies that spent money on paid ads. Win rates and sales cycle velocity (how long it took to get a new customer) were the additional metrics most used by B2B companies.

So get out your physical or virtual highlighter and pick up some great ideas for growing your company faster.

Forget about What You Learned about Marketing

We're an online marketing company, and we do very little, if any, online marketing.

—**KYLE MITNICK, Advertise Purple**

The attract phase aims to produce an ongoing supply of qualified prospects, which generally involves marketing, advertising, and branding. To be clear, I did not specifically cover business or pricing models as a strategic way of attracting customers, so our research was focused on more traditional marketing concepts.

Today, across both B2C and B2B markets, the customer has never had more power in the buying journey. There is information asymmetry, which is a fancy way of saying that most potential customers have much more information on us than we have on them.

To make matters worse, the customer journey is difficult to define since it isn't linear anymore (was it ever?). Books and consultants have talked about mapping the buyer's journey, but the problem is that it can vary from customer to customer and is rarely a consistent straight road map to a purchase. It used to be that the marketing department would start with creating an avatar—or a persona of their perfect customer. Creating avatars helps create a brand voice (what you say in your marketing), not marketing channels and strategies.

Most of our BFGs didn't do any of the traditional marketing homework that many deem essential to success. They didn't define the customer journey or create avatars. They did, however, mention having an ideal customer profile (ICP). They defined their ICP more around the problems the customer was trying to solve instead of the demographic or psychographics of their customers. I believe it's mainly because they created such tight customer communities that they deeply understood their customers at a level that their competitors did not.

The ways that prospects find you have changed dramatically. As mentioned, the traditional avatar and customer journey play a backseat role in customer intimacy and deeply understanding your customer through community engagement. The conventional buyer, both B2C and B2B, generally spends most of their research in what is known as "dark social," a term coined by Alexis Madrigal, the former editor of the *Atlantic*.

Dark social refers to informal and formal research that influences a purchase decision but is not trackable through traditional means. This could be the exchange of text messages, chats, and social DMs asking about a particular vendor or product or checking out the content on LinkedIn and comparison sites before a potential customer ever formally engages with the vendor.

Buyers of all stripes are more skeptical than ever of vendors' sales pitches. We seek to understand whether the company really gets us, and we look for social proof to give us the confidence that we're not making a buying mistake.

Our BFGs have excelled in increasing their sales because they understand their customers more deeply and the jobs to be done they are concerned with, which I discuss next.

Focus on Jobs to Be Done, Not Avatars

Where you have the data to be precise with how you talk to your customer is where you get more segmented and richer communications with them. That's where the magic happens versus defining the perfect avatar.

—LAWRENCE SCOTLAND, Creative Market

The BFG heads of marketing never mentioned using traditional marketing techniques such as avatars, jobs to be done, or other seemingly academic marketing approaches, but they did talk about ICPs, channels, and strategies. They were able to assess what their competitors weren't doing effectively enough, then test different approaches to find ways to acquire customers. They generally didn't try to compete on price or quality—they focused on being different and serving a set of unmet needs.

The BFGs knew they had to find a way to better understand what their ideal customers wanted. In some cases, their assumptions were wrong, so they either abandoned that target market segment or they tweaked their offerings. What they did figure out, even though they didn't necessarily know they were doing it, was to focus on the fundamental jobs their customers were trying to accomplish, the struggles they encountered, and the progress they sought. They were trying to understand the *why* behind their behavior, so they could discover how to attract and sell to them more effectively.

This is where the concept of jobs to be done (JTBD) comes into play. JTDB was created by Tony Ulwick, founder of the innovation consulting firm Strategyn. JTBD began as Ulwick's patented process that focused on identifying outcomes that customers seek, as opposed to products they want. Unlike traditional marketing avatars, which focus on demographic and psychographic characteristics, JTBD digs deeper into the underlying motivations and desired outcomes of the customer.

While avatars help in understanding who the customer is, JTBD focuses on what the customer wants to achieve. This difference in focus can lead to vastly different product development and marketing strategies. By identifying the job that customers are trying to get done, companies can tailor their products and marketing messages to directly address those needs, thereby increasing relevance and value in the eyes of the customer. The JTBD framework is best understood by the classic saying that "people are not interested in a drill, they are interested in a hole."

Imagine a busy professional seeking a ride. They're not simply buying a car; they're hiring a solution to the job of commuting efficiently and reliably. Recognizing this distinction is key. Understanding the job empowers businesses to create solutions that truly resonate—a self-driving car for the time-pressed professional, or a fuel-efficient option for the environmentally conscious.

By focusing on the jobs that customers need to be done, companies can move beyond traditional marketing avatars and develop products and services that truly resonate with their target audience, which is what our BFGs excelled at. The BFGs all compete in saturated and highly competitive markets where distinguishing their products and services based on features alone became challenging. It's why the Guru button that supplied twenty-four seven live help to teachers became so essential to OneScreen's success when standard touchscreen features became commoditized.

If you want to have more-effective and cost-efficient marketing strategies, use the lens of JTBD to focus on identifying both *why* and *how* your customers are looking for a solution.

Check out our Book Resources section at www.scaleupfaster.com/resources for our executive brief "The CEO's Guide to Jobs to Be Done."

Pick One Growth Lever to Master

I would say, pick your poison, but make it work. There's a bunch of different ways to grow a company. But if you use a shotgun and just cross your fingers that one of the five options you invested money in for growth will work, I think that's a poor plan.
—KYLE MITNICK, Advertise Purple

ADVERTISE PURPLE

When I started the research, I was convinced that I would find that BFGs acquired customers in a reasonably consistent way. I also assumed that they would use integrated marketing strategies and tactics across multiple channels in a sophisticated way.

Boy, was I wrong!

I was frankly shocked at hearing how differently every company approached attracting prospective customers in their market and made it work for them. This includes Advertising Purple and Freestar's maniacal focus on cold-calling prospects, Farmgirl Flowers' heavy reliance on viral branding and community, and RIVA's heavy dependence on LinkedIn organic content.

The underlying theme in all these extraordinary growth stories will be a buzzkill for companies looking for the silver bullet of customer acquisition. Each company figured out what channel and strategy worked best for them and doubled down on becoming excellent at it. Virtually all of the BFGs either started with a particular way of getting new business or kept working on it until they got it right. Many failed trying a few different strategies until they settled on the one that fit their culture. Kyle Mitnick understands the value of persistence. He told me, "We made sales work. It didn't work in the beginning, but I made it work by sheer scale and stick-to-itiveness."[2]

This is consistent with the strategy identified by Matt Lerner, founder of SYSTM and an early employee of PayPal, who was a witness to, and a key member of, many of the brands we know today. He also noted that the fastest-growing companies found a method that worked, had favorable unit economics (a fancy way of saying that their cost of acquiring new customers left them enough margin to deliver the product or service), and doubled down on making it work for them.

Alex Hormozi backs this up in his bestselling book, *$100M Leads: How to Get Strangers to Want to Buy Your Stuff*:

> Real business is messy. It takes a lot to find what audiences, lead magnets, methods, and platforms ["channels" in this book] work best. And you can only find out what works if you try. So you have to try a lot of different ways for a long enough time to know for sure.[3]

There are many ways to acquire new customers, and the endless supply of gurus will try to convince you that their way is the best. The list of what to do to acquire new customers is endless!

For instance, let's say you're convinced that organic SEO is your thing—it will be your growth lever. It takes a lot of testing, focus, and effort to become dominant in organic search. If you do it right, it doesn't take a lot of money. But neither SEO nor paid search is a game for toe dippers. You have to be committed because the competition for keywords is getting more intense, and the algorithms by Google and Microsoft keep evolving. The day I searched SEO on Google, it presented 1.7 million search results, and as usual, I never even got to page 2. (As the saying goes, page 2 is where all good search results go to die.)

To make this channel even more challenging, the introduction of AI tools like ChatGPT and Bard is completely changing the game. As the use of AI tools grows, the links you worked so hard to get on page 1, or the keywords you paid handsomely for, may not even show up in any results to a query in these tools. So, if SEO is your thing, and you're convinced that this is where you want to focus your attention and marketing dollars, play to win, and don't dabble.

The BFG companies utilized every type of customer acquisition strategy, so we know they all work, but they didn't dilute their efforts by trying to be good at several of them. Each of our BFGs found a method that worked for their culture and used that singular method to scale. There are endless strategies to attract new customers and grow faster. Pick one that best fits your culture and budget and master it. Kyle Mitnick makes a strong case for this approach:

> I think that's a big misconception with entrepreneurs who think, let me sprinkle around my marketing budget between five different channels, and one of them will work, and then I'll just go down that way. I'm more of a proponent of putting all that budget in one channel. And if you have a glimmer of success, do it repeatedly, and then you can start to optimize and refine it, which becomes your primary channel.

The way you ultimately decide whether something is the right marketing strategy for you is by measuring it and setting clear ROI-based metrics around whether it's working. Don't assume that if you don't see results right away, that means you're throwing your money away and it's not going to work. Too many business owners throw in the towel too early—they give up before they have given their customer acquisition strategy time to work and generate successes. Leverage what Kyle Mitnick calls micro-conversions, and keep working on each step of the buying journey until you know factually it's not working or it finally does. As Kyle explained:

Before you pick your poison and choose your channel, you need to have everything tracked down to each click or whatever, like what a micro-metric would be for that channel. You need full transparency and visibility into where your dollars are going, where people are stopping and jumping out of your funnel. The question of when enough is enough is when those micro conversions tell you so. If you have five steps from your outbound to your closed deal with outbound sales as your channel, you'll see where they're dropping off. If they're dropping off on the first step, and nobody's making it to the next one, you double down and spend time optimizing that one step. And the same goes for digital marketing. I think at that point, you let the data speak. I don't know many entrepreneurs obsessed enough with the micro-conversion concept to shepherd people through where they want them to go. They're like, well, I threw $5,000 on PPC, and it didn't work, so I'm moving on now. I'm going to hire a PR firm. That's typically what I hear. It makes me fall out of my chair.

Check out our Book Resources section at www.scaleupfaster.com/resources for our Growth Channel Selector (GCS), which is designed to help you decide which growth channel might be best for you.

Create and Foster Your Community

Are you a Swiftie? Part of the BeyHive or KISS Army?

Maybe you're a Little Monster, Madridista, or part of Arnie's Army.

Or possibly you are a Beatlemaniac, Cheesehead, Deadhead, Potterhead, or Parrot Head (or maybe a combination of any of these).

The point is that these are all *communities* created by fans of musicians, sports teams, and athletes. "Community" is a powerful concept and, when nurtured, it generates a flywheel of growth that can exponentially propel a company's (or an individual's) marketing investments.

Arguably, no one does this better than Taylor Swift, which is a big reason why she blew away all previous records for concert ticket sales in 2023. She carefully nurtures and connects with her community and taps into them for ideas.

What does this have to do with growing your sales faster?

A common theme across nearly every one of our BFGs was that they actively and strategically (even though some didn't know they were doing it at the time) created communities of their customers, followers, and stakeholders. As Michael Sacca, the former chief product officer for Dribbble, explained it, "I think that's always been our competitive advantage. The community just found a connection [with us], and they found a connection with each other. And because of that, the brand has value."[4]

These communities served to support each other and promote the business without them asking for help. This frequently gets measured through the NPS (which I discuss later), which posits that you can spend less money on marketing and sales if you have many customers promoting your business without you asking.

And the best case is when your community gives itself a name, like the Swifties.

Strong communities can be created in any industry, B2C or B2B. Here are a few examples.

COMMUNITY AT CLICKFUNNELS

ClickFunnels is a cloud-based software company that helps companies create fully functioning sales funnels to sell products and services online.

The company bootstrapped itself to more than $100 million in annual revenue quickly and created a rabid community of Funnel Hackers along the way. The company's cofounder and chief experience officer, Russell Brunson, and cofounder and chief strategy officer, Todd Dickerson, nurture their community as carefully as Christina Stembel and her committed team at Farmgirl Flowers do. A Funnel Hacker is a passionate (in a good way) company or person that leverages the tools from ClickFunnels to sell their products or services and sometimes the products or services of others.[5]

This community, nearly one million people strong, promotes ClickFunnels for free. (Wouldn't you like one million people pushing your company's products or services without you having to pay them?) Russell and Todd's team have done an outstanding job of creating a community of followers that leverages the cloud-based software tools they sell and creates an industry around the company.

They even created a "Funnel Hacker Manifesto" (Figure 6.1), which helps unify the community. If it sounds a bit cultish to you, that's the point. It's a rallying cry to bring people together, usually in support of the organization that nurtures it. Go to a Taylor Swift or Grateful Dead concert, and you'll see what I mean.

COMMUNITY AT FARMGIRL FLOWERS

Farmgirl Flowers is a woman-founded and women-led company that focuses on building a community of their customers (generally women). Their branding, messaging, packaging, and product selection work together to tap deeply into the zeitgeist of their customers (their community).

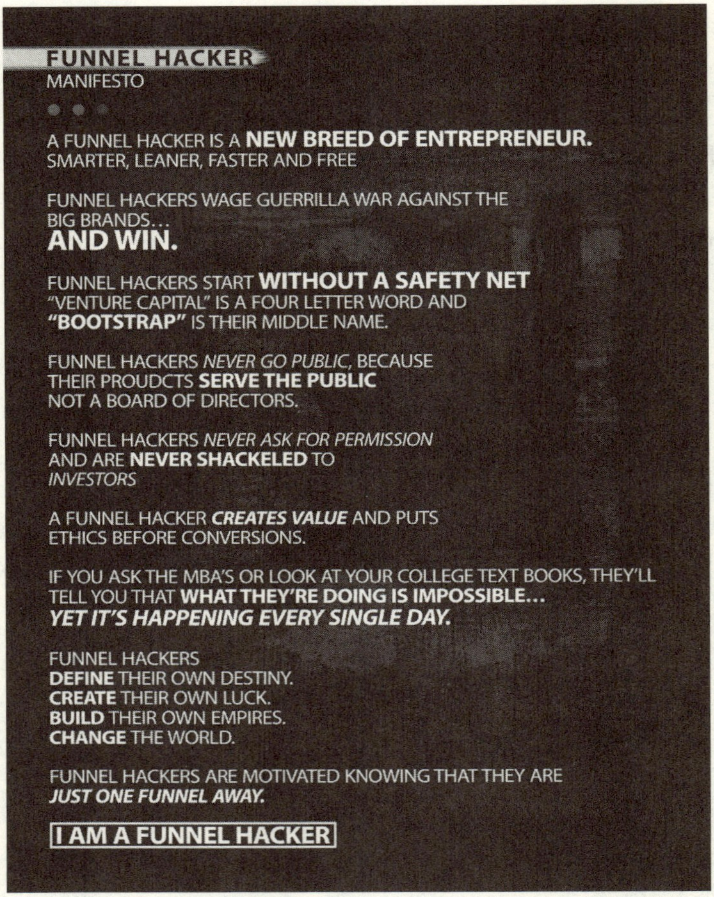

Figure 6.1. The Funnel Hacker Manifesto

According to Kat Taylor, part of the appeal of Farmgirl Flowers lies in their roots and in Christina Stembel, the company's founder:

> There's just something about her story that's really accessible to a lot of folks. We're the only large-scale e-commerce flower company that is 100 percent female-founded and majority female-run as well. There's that relationship between who's making and

> receiving the flowers because the flowers are predominantly in the female space. The other brands don't have our competitive set at this level.[6]

A concrete example of this level of customer intimacy and development of true community started with enamel pins. Farmgirl Flowers began including enamel pins in their shipments when they found that their shipping partners often damaged the flowers in their handling and delivery. As Kat told me:

> When I first started at Farmgirl, we included an enamel pin in case a stem breaks in shipping. It was a mini pin with a little note on it that said, "Accidents happen. Just in case one or two stems break in transit, we've included a couple of extra, so here's a forever bouquet on us."

There were so many social posts around the pin, they just went with it. They began including short notes from the CEO about how hard the team was working for the holidays and other related personal stories. Indeed, the more personal Christina got, the bigger the responses were. It gave people a personal connection to the people putting together the flowers—the connection went beyond a simple purchase.

Farmgirl Flowers continued engaging more deeply with their customers and began talking about life. For instance, they ran a series about how "flowers are hard, but so are a million other things." They created a little enamel pin that said "Grit" in the box of flowers, with a little note from Christina saying something like this:

> As a bootstrapped company, we know firsthand how hard some aspects of life can be because being a florist is basically like you're Sisyphus. You're rolling the same boulder up the hill a million times a day. So, if your

> personal version of your Everest is bootstrapping a business or trying to raise babies or whatever challenge you have, everybody needs a little grit. If you forget where yours is now, it's right on your lapel.[7]

The response and the number of stories and long emails they received were enormous. Customers would ask for extra pins to pass out to their friends. One group had a friend pass away from cancer, and they all wore the grit pins to that friend's funeral. Another person shared a story where they pinned it to their backpack when they were summiting Everest to memorialize their brother who had just passed away.

The key from a marketing perspective was that this was not a campaign in the traditional sense. Farmgirl Flowers profoundly understands their customers. They are authentic, and they tap into the emotions and needs of their community.

And all of this cost virtually zero dollars. They leveraged the virality of their authenticity to retain existing customers and attract new ones. This is how bootstrapped companies think creatively, engage with and nurture their community of customers, and push the sales flywheel substantially faster than their competitors with less effort and expense.

COMMUNITY AT DLP CAPITAL

DLP is a real estate development company. The founder, Don Wenner, started as a real estate agent in economically challenged Allentown, Pennsylvania. You wouldn't think an organization with $6 billion in assets under management would have anything to do with community, but they do. And it has been a significant driver of their growth.

They cleverly figured out that they could grow their business if they helped individuals and other real estate developers learn how to build a better business for themselves. DLP uses its funds to provide capital for these investors and developers and its internal real estate projects. To foster their community, they hold in-person Elite Events that help real estate investors (flippers and developers) learn how to grow their businesses faster, creating goodwill and making DLP the primary capital source of choice for those people. This is their primary marketing and growth lever, and it has helped them grow into a multibillion-dollar company. Don Wenner talked to me about their community:

> We've built this community, what we call our Elite Membership. We've got about fifty groups where we help them scale their business. When I think about the first thirteen to fourteen years of my career, I built one elite organization. But over the last few years, I've been able to focus on building fifty elite organizations by deploying our learnings, systems, resources, and capital into a bunch of other organizations.[8]

The real test of whether you have an engaged community is how many people tattoo your logo on their bodies! That's commitment, and that's engagement!

> Check out our Resources section at www.scaleupfaster.com/resources for ideas on starting and building your highly engaged community.

Double Down on What Makes You Unique—Even If It's Weird and Counterintuitive

One of the success secrets of Warren Buffett (of Berkshire Hathaway fame) is his focus on buying or investing in companies with a strategic moat. Companies with a defensible moat typically have pricing authority, resulting in higher long-term profits and richer market value.

You create a competitive moat by isolating those attributes, the elements of your product or service, that give you a defendable market position. Many think that their marketing is a competitive moat. Still, because marketing strategies are easier to copy than ever, you need to find and leverage something else that makes you unique—and sometimes you can be known for the smallest things that matter to customers.

The strategic framework to do this is called lighthouse positioning, and you can achieve it in one of two ways (most companies will do a bit of both):

1. Truly build a better mousetrap (offering) that sets you apart.
2. Be way better at marketing than your competitors.

But to ensure your lighthouse positioning will work, it must achieve both of these things:

1. Make you unique.
2. Be something customers genuinely care about!

Once you have your Lighthouse Positioning in place that leverages your point of differentiation, you need to create a customer acquisition or buyer enablement process that resets the buying criteria in your favor. (I'll give you some examples from our BFGs.) In other words, you need to put your prospective customer in a position in their mind where you are the only option to solve their problem.

Let's dig into this more by looking at some of our beloved BFGs. Imagine buying flowers for yourself or a loved one, but you don't get to pick the type! Sound crazy? Would you do it?

How about buying a mattress, but to even check them out, you can only book a specific time to see them, and you have to go to a warehouse, not a retail store. Would you buy from them?

Or you're interested in increasing the advertising sales for your website, and in doing so, you must literally give up virtually all control of your site. Yeah, right, not doing it!

As crazy as a few of these offerings seem, Farmgirl Flowers, RSS (via their BoxDrop franchise), and Freestar have all executed these unique market positions to achieve remarkable growth. They all leaned into these competitive market positions that probably seemed crazy at the time. Still, they had to find a way to create truly unique and sustainable market positions and, along the way, have achieved outsized gross margins (ah, just what Warren is looking for).

Christina Stembel talked with me about the early days at Farmgirl Flowers:

> When I started, it was a completely new idea—you not getting to pick the flowers. The only thing that they have to do is look pretty, right? And convey that you're loved. That's it. I didn't know if they'd give up the choice. And you know, our competitors had 169 options or more on their website. We had one, so it was a novel concept.

I call this Lighthouse Positioning because it serves as a distinct beacon of customer value in a sea of sameness.

> Check out our Resources section at www.scaleupfaster.com/resources for how to do a competitive positioning analysis on the path to creating your Lighthouse Positioning.

Chapter 7

ACQUIRE (SALES)

KEY INSIGHTS

- Measure and refine your sales process, whether an e-commerce funnel or a complex B2B direct sales process, until you master it.
- Stop selling and leverage storytelling using data to add value to the buying process.
- Be way more transparent than you're comfortable with—the trust you earn will win you more deals than you'll lose.

Using our original example of the stalls at the market, how do you get them to buy something once you get a prospect to visit *your* stall? That's what this chapter is all about—how our BFGs do an outstanding job of getting customers to take out their credit cards, write the purchase order, and buy products and services from them versus their competitors.

In fact, how would you like to close 90 percent of all the prospects who walk through the door? Would you settle for 80 percent?

A few of our BFGs have mastered the direct sales process for B2C and B2B. One company I tell you about is so successful that they patented their sales process!

Measure, Master, Refine, and Then Scale

The companies that have mastered selling tirelessly measure and refine their sales process. RSS, through their BoxDrop franchise, where they sell mattresses and furniture, has a closing rate of nearly 90 percent from when a prospective customer enters their warehouse location through objection-handling and successful closing. This is partially due to how they go to market, how they presell the customer, and their by-appointment-only model. They constantly measure every step of the buying process, monitor it, and refine it to ensure the end-to-end process is as successful as possible. Once they dialed in their process, they rolled it out to all their franchisees. Jerry Williams, the president of RSS, explained their process to me:

> From the sales process, it's all scripted out. Nothing happens by accident when you first walk into one of our locations. We set up the showroom and greet you at the door in an exact way; we say the same thing each time. And we have the answer to every question they ask. We already know our response to direct the customer in a certain way or to a certain product and can step you up that product line. We track everything from conversions to what percentage of the time there are no-shows. If the customer is a no-show more than 10 percent of the time, we know we're doing or saying something wrong. If we don't close a mattress sale more than 80 percent or 90 percent of the time, there's something wrong in our sales process. The average mattress store would be lucky to get a 25 percent close ratio; we're at 90 percent plus.[1]

This type of refined process is precisely what you should do to grow faster and scale predictably and profitably. I see too many business owners hiring salespeople without a proven process, assuming that a great salesperson will figure it out if they're good enough. Hiring a salesperson is generally the most expensive sales or marketing investment you can make, so it behooves you to figure out a sales process that *measurably* works before you hire too many salespeople, whether they are inside or outside field salespeople. Start small, measure, refine, and master. Then scale up.

At Advertise Purple, they chose direct sales as their primary channel. It was tough going at first, because this was not how their competitors did it. Their competitors attended all the conferences, fought for the awards, and sold through relationship building via the old boys' network. Fortunately, Advertise Purple recognized that this model isn't scalable. They took a different path, and using a data-centric selling approach, they started dialing for dollars. This strategy worked so well that they have thousands of customers rather than the dozens their largest competitors have.

Advertise Purple developed a two-stage sales process, and they worked hard on each step, resulting in an 80 percent conversion rate from their stage 1 to stage 2 sales flow. They manage their prospecting on a thirty-day rolling cycle where their business development representatives receive their outreach objectives every thirty days from a database of 350,000 prospects, and then they reach out and prospect (stage 1). Stage 2 involves further qualification, education, follow-up, and closing. The results speak for themselves with an industry-high close rate. They work on refining this process constantly, and it has contributed to the extraordinary growth they've experienced.

JCW Group also leverages a direct sales model, and they have established a training academy to teach the process. Their sales process is focused on adding value from the very first conversation. So many organizations say they do this, but they're just pitching when you look into the sales conversations. As an outcome of the measured care they provide through their Customer Care Charter, JCW also does a great job of expanding every account. Even if an account isn't active, they track the regular follow-ups that their team does. They track calls, meetings, and follow-ups and regularly audit an individual salesperson's performance. Their sales teams don't take offense to the reporting because they know they make more money when they follow their proven process!

Get Naked—Show Them Your Flaws Up Front

What do you do first when you're looking for a restaurant, a place to go, or a thing to buy online? You probably look at the customer reviews. Most people do.

We are skeptical, so when we see the reviews and a perfect rating of 5 out of 5, we assume the reviews are fake. When we see anything lower than a 4 out of 5, we'll probably move on. The average customer rating that statistically drives new business is between 4.2 and 4.6 out of a possible 5. (I don't know about you, but I first look at the 1 and 2 ratings to see whether the comments are inconsequential or from impossibly demanding people and how and whether the business responded. If the 1s and 2s aren't related to the product or service, only then do I look at the positive ratings.)

What do online customer ratings have to do with transparency?

If there are customer reviews for your business on the web (I assume there are), you'll be fighting uncontrolled perception from the beginning. Most people assume there might be issues—they want to know that you'll acknowledge mistakes and actively fix them. That's why we're most likely to purchase when the rating is a 4.6 and not a 5; it seems truthful and trustworthy. We're all wired to look for social proof (customer reviews) in every purchase, and we're all wired to be skeptical of vendor claims (all 5 ratings).

With that in mind, could you imagine having a business tell you what was wrong with their product or service or why customers didn't buy from them on your first interaction? This is how some of our BFGs sell more effectively—through more transparency.

Transparency is undoubtedly a process that requires finesse, but some of our BFGs have transparency built into their sales process. Whether it's B2B or B2C, it's refreshing for a business to be open about potential product or service issues that will arise or have arisen in the past and how they were handled. It sounds unbelievable that a business would bring up objections from the very beginning, but doing so builds trust.

As detailed in the book *Transparency Sale*, by my friend and former colleague Todd Caponi, something as counterintuitive as leading with your flaws can result in faster sales cycles, increased win rates, and an unstoppable competitive edge. He posits that transparency and vulnerability in your presentations and negotiations lead to faster and larger deals, faster payments, longer commitments, and more predictable sales forecasts.[2]

As Todd explains in his book, a few of our BFGs used this as a selling strategy where they don't just hide their flaws—they lay them out for a prospect to evaluate. This does two things: It reduces the typical sales resistance and builds trust right out of the gate. Surprisingly, telling prospects both the good and the bad about your product results in closing more sales quickly.

Focus on Long-Term Relationships

Everyone knows the age-old adage about how much easier and less expensive it is to sell to a current customer than acquire a new one. How many companies invest in a selling process for generating more revenue post-purchase?

Freestar has figured this out. They have a negative churn rate, meaning they replace any revenue from customers that churn with new incremental revenue from existing accounts. To do this, they have a professional post-sales team whose goal is to grow each account and increase their monthly revenue from their customers. They do that with various approaches, ultimately producing additional revenue for their customers, so it's mutually beneficial. Many companies do a fine job of customer service. Still, they don't think strategically enough about increasing the back-end revenue streams where the acquisition cost is virtually zero and the sales velocity is faster.

Let's explore this concept a bit more deeply. Would you spend millions of dollars selling a product you lose money on? ClickFunnels does. Let me explain.

ClickFunnels has developed a sales strategy that generates enough front-end revenue to pay for their advertising costs (called a self-liquidating ad) and then get the customer into a buying habit by up-selling a high-value, low-cost product. This then kicks into a back-end process that sells their core product offer for a lot more money (at virtually zero incremental cost).

ClickFunnels achieves this by buying paid traffic ads that send people to a specific landing page. When you hit their landing page, they ask for your email address in exchange for a free gift—sometimes called a lead magnet. ClickFunnels gives away something of much higher value than most lead magnets, and as a result, they typically achieve a 20 percent opt-in rate for the free gift.

Then, this is where the financial magic happens.

Once you opt-in for the free gift, on the thank you page, they offer a $7 product (an upsell), which typically converts around 10 percent of potential customers. They have fully paid for their advertising costs based on these opt-in and conversion rates. Every additional dollar of sales they collect is pure gross profit.

They first focus on getting their front-end acquisition engine effective enough to pay for their advertising costs, and then they focus their attention on the long-tail back-end revenue of their core product. At that point, they are selling to current customers with higher trust, resulting in higher close rates and lower nominal sales spending.

Imagine if you could do this in your business. Your marketing budget would then be infinite. This simple and effective strategy is why ClickFunnels has grown so rapidly. In the ClickFunnels example, even though the per-transaction sales numbers seem small, this is massive leverage at scale.

Here's how the math on this strategy works.

It costs ClickFunnels around $27 in ad spend (plus the cost of shipping) to give away one of their free books (they have to pay shipping and handling), which is a low-cost, high-value offer. Based on the conversion and opt-in rates, each prospect who moves through their online book funnel is worth an average of $35 per person when all front- and back-end sales are collected (you see—spend $27, get $35). Once they have a new customer, even for the low-cost offers, the percentage of customers who ultimately subscribe to their cloud-based marketing platform is very high. They make thousands of dollars in profit per customer over the customer lifecycle. Consequently, ClickFunnels can afford to run campaigns at breakeven because the back-end revenue pays off in spades. This strategy has been modeled by many other companies, especially in the online space, so think about how you can use a similar approach in your business.

This front- and back-end revenue model is one of the reasons they were recently offered $1 billion in cash for the company—which the founders rejected. (They love what they do too much to sell—crazy, I know!)

> Check out our Resources section at www.scaleupfaster.com/resources for our ebook *The Automatic Customer*, which includes a list of how you can create recurring revenue streams for your business (which will add substantial value to your company).

Your Zero-Cost, Top-Performing Sales Force

What if you could have dozens, hundreds, or even thousands of top-performing salespeople work for you for free? And what if these salespeople are exceptional at finding new business for you? Would you be interested?

Of course you would. Who wouldn't?

You can build this super-sized superstar sales force by providing world-class service to your customers so that they promote your company and brand to their friends and colleagues. Let your customers sell for you; you can spend less on marketing and sales than your competitors. I'm not talking about asking a few customers to be a reference in the B2B sense or incentivizing your B2C customers to leave a positive review. I'm talking about providing a product and service of such exceptional quality that you don't need to ask; they do it of their own volition—they become a promoter.

The concept of a customer as your promoter was developed by Fred Reichheld in 2000 through his *New York Times* bestseller *The Ultimate Question 2.0*. Fred posits that customer loyalty is about much more than repeat purchases.[3] Even someone who repeatedly buys from the same company may be open to alternatives if a better deal or a product with newer features is presented. And sometimes a product doesn't fall into the repeat purchases category. If a competitor calls one of your loyal customers, the customer will shut them down almost immediately. If a customer isn't that loyal, they'll pay attention to see whether switching brands is worth their while.

You can also tell whether a person is a promoter if they talk your ear off about a brand or product you didn't even ask about—like Apple people. (Yeesh—I'm an Android guy.)

When a company has a higher percentage of "promoters," the customers are selling on their behalf, so they can spend less on customer acquisition and thus should have higher net profits. This theory has held true; virtually every company with the highest NPSs in their industry also has higher profitability.

I have used the NPS in my companies, and most of the BFGs I spoke with did, too. A few of our BFGs had world-class NPS scores. Hence, if you trust the research, a high NPS (lots of promoters and very few detractors) leads to faster growth and higher profits (let's assume a level of causation here). It behooves you first to measure the loyalty of your customers and then work on improving every aspect of the customer experience to increase it continually. Kurt Donnell made this statement about NPS metrics:

> NPS is one of our biggest measurements that we look at every single day and every month. When I first started here, we were at about fifty. We changed the whole process of customer success and how the team functions, and next year, we hit seventy-five. We survey our customer base once a month, asking for feedback on how Freestar is doing for them. Our goal as a company is to have a seventy-five NPS, which is considered world-class.[4]

One of the most challenging things about driving customer loyalty is operationalizing the customer touchpoints across all business functions. For instance, you could have a fantastic product your customers love, but the billing or service is lousy. We should assume that every interaction, whether in person, on the phone, or on the web, affects how customers feel about your company and brand.

Because most people are influenced somewhat or primarily by their incentive plans, we found a way at the consulting firm I founded to make customer loyalty a broad measure everyone was incentivized to work on. We built a compensation plan to maximize each person's variable bonus if they helped the company have a higher NPS score. With employee input, we created a matrixed plan where individuals would be paid the maximum bonus if the customer was a promoter for them individually (in the consulting work they performed for the client) and the company. The bonus would be smaller if the customer was a promoter for them personally but not for the company.

The unintended positive benefit of this plan was that employees were much more active in raising issues that came up in other departments. For instance, when salespeople hear about a billing issue that is frustrating a customer, how often do they bring the issue to the correct department when they're only compensated on new revenue? Before this plan, our salespeople didn't communicate these types of issues within my company. After the implementation of our plan, they always did!

David Freedman, the cofounder of Freestar, talked with me about their obsession with customer service:

> In the beginning days, we had about 50 percent churn. So I don't think you call that a business, right? That's just a very leaky bucket. You have to keep filling the customer bucket just to tread water. You can talk about customer service all you want, but if the customer is not feeling it, then you've got a problem. So we started obsessing over our NPS score, but more importantly, obsessing over it and integrating the score directly into our internal Slack. Every single time any publisher gives us a score from one to ten, there's no hiding from it. Everyone in the company sees it. We've always had people who cared, but sometimes, the customer didn't have the appropriate channel to voice their concerns. Now, we could address that problem. Obviously, I strive for all ten, but when we get a four

or five, it's the comments they put in because it's usually like, wow, this is a really good point; we need to address this. And it's great watching our team jump in there and say, "I already sent an email out, and yes, we screwed this up. We're fixing it.[5]

Check out our Resources section at www.scaleupfaster.com/resources for more information on the Net Promoter Score and how to deploy it in your company.

Chapter 8

NURTURE (SERVICE)

KEY INSIGHTS

- Superior service will let your customers replace your sales team.
- Stop the bleeding of customer churn.

In the previous chapter, I talk about turning your customers into promoters to help accelerate and effectively fund faster growth. In this chapter, I detail one primary way to do that. You need to provide not just good but exceptional service that exceeds the kind your industry provides. In most cases, this is *very* easy to implement; it just takes commitment, alignment, and the right team of people who genuinely care about your customers.

Superior Service Will Let Your Customers Replace Your Sales Team

Let's start with the recruiting and staffing company JCW Group. In many cases, the word *recruiter* might bring up images that aren't particularly good. But JCW knew the perception of staffing companies in their industry and set out to professionalize the industry through hiring, training, adding value, and providing exceptional service, which propelled the company's fast and sustainable growth.

Their strategic weapon is called their Customer Care Charter, a list of the promises they make to their clients and their candidates. For example, they make sure they call each candidate they are working with at least once weekly to update them on the job application. If you've ever been a job candidate, you know how infrequently most companies communicate with you and how often you've been ghosted when the position was filled. JCW recruiters check in with their candidates every seventy-two hours to let them know how the search is going for the assignment. JCW Group's chief revenue officer, John Newton, explained their approach to me:

> For example, on a Friday afternoon, people have an hour in their diary dedicated to calling every candidate they haven't processed to update them, even to say, "I'm sorry, we have no feedback for you yet. I promise you I'm chasing it." If you do that to a candidate, you will be the only candidate recruitment company out of the other twenty they're working with that made that call, which means they'll remember and want to work with us and refer us to other candidates and clients.[1]

These are strict rules of engagement inside the company, and they expect every salesperson to comply with them. The performance metrics under their Customer Care Charter are tracked as closely as any sales performance measures. The sales reps understand that even though taking time out to complete these tasks may take time away from making quota, they know that in the long run, this level of service will pay off in more and better business. They've been trained to keep their promises, keep in touch, communicate effectively, and be prepared. In short, they've been trained to build solid relationships.

Does your company look for service skills when looking for salespeople?

Brill Media is a programmatic advertising firm that helps companies lower their costs and improve the effectiveness of leads and sales from digital marketing. One of the most significant factors in customer happiness and loyalty in this industry is how quickly the customer sees results. In other words, I'm not a happy customer if I spend advertising money but don't see any new leads or sales for weeks or months. Consequently, one of their most important processes is the customer onboarding process.

In many instances in project-type industries like Brill Media's, the sales team is working with a prospect for a long while (weeks, months, or years), and the minute they sign the contract to become a customer, the salesperson is nowhere to be found. The customer is thrown over the fence by the operations or support team. But Brill Media went to great lengths to ensure this didn't happen to their customers, as former COO Linda Monsour explained to me:

> We have our onboarding team guiding the entire process. They partner and work closely with our support engineers, pub ops, yield, and sales teams because we need them to collaborate and tell us what was discussed in the sales process. We have a full collaboration team involved in onboarding with the goal of getting them live as fast as possible.[2]

How to Stop the Bleeding (Customer Churn)

ClickFunnels has mastered measuring and testing virtually every aspect of their business. In the early days, they were experiencing a significant churn of customers who had signed up for their sales funnel software, so they wanted to see what they could do to stem the bleeding. As I discussed earlier, they spend a significant amount of money acquiring new customers, so every customer who didn't continue with their subscription (most signed up for a free trial) reduced their ROAS and increased their CAC.

The ClickFunnels team got together and decided to build what is probably considered the first cancellation funnel. Todd Dickerson told Russell Brunson, "We have funnels for people coming into ClickFunnels, why don't we have funnels for people going out of ClickFunnels?"[3]

They developed a unique way to slow down and make you think about canceling their service without feeling like it was impossible to cancel. (This was unlike most subscription services—try to cancel your cable company!) They did this without leaving a bad taste in your mouth or inviting scrutiny from the Better Business Bureau or the Federal Trade Commission.

The cancellation funnel involved a few steps, including the following:

- Step 1: A video from Russell Brunson with a menu from which you could select the reason you are canceling. (They aggregate and evaluate this data to improve the product.)
- Step 2: They know that most people don't renew because they didn't take the time to learn about the product, so there are several options for additional training or the ability to make money by becoming an affiliate. At this point, you can either pause or cancel your account.
- Step 3: If you cancel, they remind you that all your data will be deleted unless you pause your account for a nominal fee.
- Step 4: If you still choose to cancel, there's a visual of the domain and data you used through their system, which shows a big red X reminding you that you cannot access any of it if you cancel.

This simple and customer-friendly four-step process cut their churn rate by 50 percent!

The point is that very few companies think about the offboarding of customers who may want to cancel for legitimate reasons. It's not always that your customer isn't happy or doesn't like your product. So focus first on creating a fantastic onboarding process, then on a sustainable nurturing process, then experiment with developing a pre-churn process to potentially save those customers you want to keep.

Chapter 9

CO-INNOVATE

KEY INSIGHT

- Customers will tell you exactly how to grow—if you listen.

The final part of our customer process is the co-development of new products and services with your customers. Many companies take customer feedback and either don't do anything with the input or make only incremental improvements to their product or service.

I'm talking about working closely with your customers and your community to invent new products and services that serve them better. Doing this effectively means you must be 100 percent market-focused. You need to be great at listening to direct customer feedback and, more importantly, customer cues.

As discussed earlier, most of our BFGs effectively ignored their competition and created their own path forward. They could do this because they deeply understood their markets—either because they were their own customers like Farmgirl Flowers or because they had a customer feedback loop and engagement process to learn what the market was actively looking for. As Christina Fiasconaro, Freestar's executive vice president of supply, told me, "We've had a lot of conversations with publishers who have come to us with a product idea or solution, or said it would be great if you guys could do this. We take that back to our product team, and they start putting it on their road map."[1]

The biggest differentiator for our BFG OneScreen was their Guru button, which is embedded in their touchscreen product(s) and provides free, unlimited help and training. This was their differentiator, because technology adoption can be difficult in their marketplace where they sell to K–12 teachers and administrators. This technology was built as a fundamental feature in their product because they had a feedback loop and listened to their customers.

Sufian Munir, the CEO of OneScreen, told me that they saw so many electronic whiteboards in classrooms with layers of dust from non-use that they started asking their customers why they weren't being used. They discovered through many conversations that their customers "have this technology in the classroom, but they have nobody to teach them how to use it. They have nobody to support them, so they don't use it. You know, especially in front of students, they're too shy to use technology."[2] Furthermore, the schools had virtually no technical support to help them. The teachers didn't have the time to get lots of training and didn't want to appear ignorant in front of their students.

To solve this problem, Sufian told me they "hired a small team of engineers, put a Guru button on the screen, and said, 'Okay, anytime you need help, teachers, press this button. It will initiate a video call with our support team, and they will train you impromptu and on demand whenever you want.'" The Guru button is a free and easy-to-use support structure built into their product that helped OneScreen compete more effectively, take market share, and grow faster. The people on the receiving end of those calls are not customer service reps; they're product engineers who can help with any big or small issue immediately.

PART III

Capital

protect →
grow →
leverage →
reinvest

Revenue is vanity, profit is sanity,
and cash flow is king.

—VERNE HARNISH, *SCALING UP*

Most business owners and CEOs I speak with about the health of their business tend to focus on revenue, profit, or maybe the number of employees (most VC-backed companies concentrate on the number of employees!) Virtually none of them talk about the free cash flow they generate, even though most business owners generally know this is perhaps the most important performance metric. They understand that their ability to generate positive cash flow makes the difference between high growth and going out of business.

I can't read a cash flow statement—and neither could they! I have an MBA in finance, but a traditional accounting cash flow statement may as well be in hieroglyphics because it makes no sense to me—and I know I'm not alone. This isn't unique to our BFGs, of course. Most business owners learn more about the income statement and balance sheet even though business valuations and capital financing rely more on cash generation. It is likely because they do not understand precisely how cash flows in their business, how their day-to-day decisions affect the cash position, or even which levers will move the needle. Understanding how cash flows in your business, and more importantly how to manage it, will help you scale without having to seek external capital.

Neelu Modali, the COO of RIVA Solutions, has the same attitude toward a cash flow statement that I have. But he has a deep knowledge of how cash actually flows in the business:

> I've always found the health of the business is based on the behavior of money, the behavior of the cash, and it's not like cash flow. I don't, and I can't, read a balance sheet. I'm not somebody who can put all this stuff together and dissect it for you. What I can tell you is that I do understand how to take an A/R report, a P&L, and a balance sheet and map it to the deposits that are

> happening on a real-time basis to be able to tell you whether or not this company is going to be alive next month or next quarter. So understanding that behavior of money enables me to put a finger to the air and really operate the business.[1]

The BFG CEOs I spoke to admitted that they hired their CFO or finance vice president (one of the last leadership positions hired) because they needed to manage cash better as their businesses got more complex. They felt that they needed someone better than themselves. A few admitted that they should have hired a finance leader sooner, but in general, they were growing fast enough to work through it. I heard many stories of early cash flow issues that were solved through credit cards, company leaders pitching in, customer and vendor financing, or invoice factoring.

With this backdrop, I discuss how our BFGs have funded their exceptional growth by staying lean, watching expenses, pricing performance, creativity, and a little luck. I break down this part into four chapters focused on the role of cash during the various stages a company goes through as it grows and scales.

The first chapter, "Protect," details some strategies the companies used to manage their cash flow tightly until they reached the point of consistently positive cash flow. The second chapter, "Grow," is when our BFGs began to understand how they could generate more cash than their growth needed and began to build a war chest that served them as they accelerated their growth. The third chapter briefly touches on when they decided to pursue leverage to give them the flexibility to scale faster without tapping into their cash reserves. Finally, I discuss how our BFGs reinvested into their businesses to improve their valuations and put them into a position to make strategic investments.

Chapter 10

PROTECT

We were always focused on our profit and loss statement. But cash flow was not a regularly discussed topic. It was as if we were driving along, watching only the speedometer, when in fact we were running out of gas.

—ATTRIBUTED TO MICHAEL DELL

KEY INSIGHTS

- Calculate and track your cash conversion cycle on a daily or weekly basis.
- Focus on improving your cash conversion cycle.

Cash truly is king, and one of the best ways to understand how your company is doing is by measuring your cash conversion cycle (CCC). As Verne Harnish says, "Cash is the oxygen that fuels growth. And the cash conversion cycle (CCC) is a key performance indicator (KPI) that measures how long it takes for a dollar spent on anything (rent, utilities, marketing, payroll, etc.) to make its way through your business and back into your pocket."[1] I don't particularly like the name of this financial metric. Still, it can transform a business's operational dynamics, offering a pathway to growth without the reliance on external capital.

Albert Einstein, it is said, revered compound interest as the "eighth wonder of the world," a principle that underlines the power of investment growth over time. In a parallel vein, the CCC can be considered the ninth wonder in the business domain, especially for companies that want to grow and scale faster without raising external capital.

An Explanation of the Cash Conversion Cycle

Before I get into our BFG's CCCs, let me help you better understand why the concept is essential and how it's measured. Simply put, the CCC calculates the period between outlaying cash to fulfill a customer order and when you receive the money from the customer. If you receive the cash for the product before you have to spend money to deliver it, you have a negative CCC. If you spend money on inventory and personnel before you get the cash, you have a positive CCC. So, in this case, negative is good, and positive is bad. (I bet that's the first time you've heard that!)

Let's explore this concept further.

The CCC comprises three metrics:

1. *Days inventory outstanding (DIO):* This is the average duration to sell inventory. DIO for service businesses is replaced with days work in progress (DWIP) or days service outstanding. This measures the time it takes to complete a service or project. It can be challenging to quantify, but it is essential for understanding how efficiently a company delivers its services.

2. *Days sales outstanding (DSO):* This is still a critical component and is calculated similarly for goods and services companies. It measures the average number of days it takes for a company to collect payment after a service or product has been sold and delivered. It's calculated by dividing the ending accounts receivable by the total credit sales and multiplying by the period's number of days.
3. *Days payables outstanding (DPO):* This represents the average number of days a company takes to pay its bills and invoices from suppliers. It's calculated by dividing ending accounts payable by the number of days in the period.

Product-based cash conversion cycle =
Days inventory outstanding + Days sales outstanding –
Days payables outstanding

Services-based cash conversion cycle =
Days service outstanding + Days sales outstanding –
Days payables outstanding

A negative CCC indicates a company sells and collects customer payments before settling its bills with suppliers or pays out for the services delivered (payroll or external contractors). This scenario essentially means customers and suppliers are financing the company's operations, allowing it to grow without an additional cash infusion. Conversely, a positive CCC necessitates ongoing cash input to fuel business expansion. Although the calculation looks complex, it's straightforward to do once you have the inputs, and many accounting packages can calculate this automatically.

The average CCC for our BFGs was negative five point two (–5.2), and the median was negative six point five (–6.5), which partially explains why these companies could grow and scale fast without raising external capital. In other words, they had on average 5.2 days of positive cash flow as they grew and scaled. This doesn't sound like much cushion, but when you have tens or hundreds of millions of dollars in sales, this is significant.

Most of our BFGs didn't start with these exceptional numbers but understood the importance of self-funding the business, so they constantly worked on improving in this area. Kurt Donnell told me that this was one of the first things he worked on when he joined Freestar. He said, "When I got here, our float was backwards. Our receivables were forty-eight days, and our payables averaged forty-five or something like that. I very quickly went and fixed this when I got here. I've got payables and receivables solidly five to seven days in the right direction."[2] Clearly, Kurt understood the significance of this metric.

Focus on Improving Your Cash Conversion Cycle

Like our BFGs, you should never stop working on finding ways to create a negative CCC to fund your growth and scale. There are countless strategies to achieve this level of capital efficiency, but here are a few:

1. Create strategic supplier relationships to minimize inventory levels. Efficient inventory management reduces cash outlays and holding costs, lead times, and inventory levels, and accelerates your cash conversion process. These are all crucial for businesses dependent on external manufacturing.
2. Reduce your DSO. Encourage prepayment or early payment through preorders or subscription models to lower DSO significantly and bolster cash flow. Farmgirl Flowers grew so quickly because, as an e-commerce company, the customer pays in

advance for their products. Brandon Green told me this was a key part of Dribbble's strategy:

> We did everything we could to ensure that we were collecting cash as quickly as possible with as little risk as possible, and then paying out cash at the maximum terms possible. On the credit side, at the beginning, there were no exceptions. . . . We were cash upfront for everything—any product we sold. All of our subscriptions were paid annually. We would receive a lot of money upfront for the subscription to any enterprise-level services. If you didn't pay before the run date of your campaign or advertising, we wouldn't run it. So the carrot was that you had to book your inventory and pay ahead of time. We really minimized the risk of nonpayment and bad debt.[3]

3. Extend your DPO. Negotiating favorable payment terms with suppliers strengthens the company's cash position, enabling reinvestment and growth without immediate outlays. RSS grew so quickly because they worked closely with vendors to improve their trade credit terms from cash up front to fifteen days and, eventually, to longer payment terms once trust was built. Many companies don't renegotiate supplier terms once they are established, so review your terms with key suppliers every year. As Scott Andrew explained to me, this approach worked well for RSS:

> We worked directly with vendors and traveled to meet with them face-to-face to tell them our ideas, where we believe we could go, and why. And we were able to establish deal terms in the first year and a half. We had

> to pay cash when we placed orders for furniture. We negotiated away with our biggest vendor to have trade credit. So we strategically created a position where we had positive cash flow.[4]

4. Develop better project management and invoicing practices. For service companies, especially those in consulting, legal, or IT services, managing the time to deliver services (DWIP or DSO) and the collection period (DSO) efficiently can significantly affect their cash flow. Optimizing DSO through better project management and invoicing practices and negotiating longer DPO terms with suppliers (for any goods or external services purchased) can help service businesses improve their cash flow and reduce the need for external financing. My consulting firm used to negotiate favorable terms with external contractors where we paid our contractors within five days of receipt of customer funds. Brandon Green explained that this was a key part of Dribbble's strategy:

> On the expense side, we've trailed our AP as long as possible, depending on whatever terms we negotiated. We didn't lock into multiyear contracts in case we needed to pivot tools. We didn't take advantage of some of the cost reductions of multiyear contracts specifically because they required upfront payments. It's something that we don't see moving away from.

There are many books that focus on improving cash flow and are chock full of ideas for you to implement in your business. By picking one strategy per week to implement, you can create a sustainable cash-flow-positive business (negative CCC) that you can use to scale and grow faster while keeping control over your destiny. The most important thing to do to create positive cash flow is to stop saying, "This is how it's done in our industry."

In one of my previous consulting firms, we sold a project to Apple, which typically demands ninety-day payment terms—because they're Apple. But my company asked for thirty-day customer payment terms in our contracts. When we first talked to them about their ridiculous payment terms, we reminded them that they were actually the "First Bank of Apple," since they had a bigger cash position back then (2012) than most large banks (Apple has $74 billion in cash and cash equivalents on hand as of December 2023).

After we hurled that insult and they got over it, we began negotiating. Although the back-and-forth negotiation delayed our sales cycle by a few months because they kicked, screamed, and told us it required approval from an executive vice president, we held firm and ultimately compromised at forty-five days. Because this was a large multiyear project, we would never have been able to fund our growth if we had agreed to their initial terms. Simon Elsbury, the former finance director for JCW Group, described a similar approach taken by that firm:

> This happens all the time. You end up with a high-volume account, and you're like, oh my God, we need to drop our trousers to get more deals. We held firm the entire time. Even when they mentioned discount, we're like, no, can't do that. We're a small company . . . essentially, don't bully us. Believe it or not, it worked. So the first thing is, make sure you're making enough profit. And I'm talking gross margin at the top.[5]

The point here is that you may need to concede in some areas (time, delivery, etc.) or find a way to provide additional value, but it's worth the effort.

Many of our BFGs took the same approach. They refused to accept industry practices when finding ways to improve cash flow and focused on adding more value in exchange for better terms. Our BFGs focused on generating revenue and preserving cash flow—constantly. And even though some of them have hundreds of millions of dollars in revenue, they still operate this way.

Check out our Resources section at www.scaleupfaster.com/resources for a list of cash-producing strategies you can use immediately to improve your cash position.

Chapter 11

MULTIPLY

Cash becomes even more critical as the business scales up, since "growth sucks cash." The key is innovating ways to generate sufficient profit and cash flow internally, so you don't have to turn to banks (or sharks!) to fuel your growth.

—VERNE HARNISH, *SCALING UP*

KEY INSIGHTS

- Create a culture of cash awareness by creating practices that positively affect cash flow.
- To grow faster and generate positive cash flow, focus on pricing authority.

Create a Culture of Cash Awareness

In the early years . . . our priority was to manage our cash very effectively—to multiply and maximize it and grow trade credit as fast as we could.

—SCOTT ANDREW, Retail Service Systems

Each one of the BFGs, regardless of their size, created a companywide culture of frugality and cash preservation. They were very up-front with their desire to be in control of their destiny by bootstrapping their growth, so they effectively brought everyone on board with them. Brandon Green told me about Dribbble's consistent and clear desire to fund their own growth:

> It's been great from the hiring perspective. It sets the tone for employees coming on that there's no big checkbook behind this. We're all working together to make this work. We're in charge of our own destiny. We don't have a big equity player, a bank breathing down our neck on covenants, or anything blocking us.

None of the Dribbble team members I spoke with ever suggested the company was cheap. Team members generally felt that their company spent money in the right places at the right time. Because many of these companies conducted many marketing and product tests where the money spent on the tests may be perceived as wasted when the results are not what they wanted, I expected to hear comments about spending money on projects that didn't pan out. But the opposite was true. Employees believed testing was paramount to continued growth and felt spending money on tests was appropriate.

In my experience, many CEOs and founders are reluctant to be vulnerable and open about the company's cash position and the need to buckle down from time to time. This was rarely an issue with our

BFG CEOs. They leaned into the need to broadly communicate the company's cash position without disclosing financials to get everyone to do their part to help the company generate more cash. Kurt Donnell described how this attitude influenced the culture at Freestar:

> Not a lot of frills, no big office, pool table, or video game room. . . . The employees sit down and say, we're all here to work, and it was fun. Everyone was on the same page with "we're being scrappy." So I think that if you have access to cash, either through equity or debt, you lose that kind of tenacity and the fight for growth.

Focus on Pricing Authority

Growing and scaling faster generally consumes cash as the business hires people, buys inventory, and adds capacity to handle the growth. Growing businesses face the dual challenge of managing day-to-day operations and funding expansion efforts. The BFGs had to perform this dance repeatedly; as they doubled revenues each year, they had to ensure that they remained cash flow positive and stayed ahead of their growth demands.

During these growth and scale phases, many of them contemplated raising external capital as cash became tighter. This is common, and many companies opt to take on growth capital from PE or VC firms. Some of our BFGs tried. Farmgirl Flowers wanted to accelerate their rapid growth, so they tried raising money, but it was not meant to be. Christina Stembel shared the saga with me:

> It was not a choice. I tried to raise capital twice. I got 104 noes and still have the spreadsheet! But you know, I can handle a lot of risk. I can eat ramen for long periods

> of time; I have backup plans, like going to work at Starbucks at night if I need to. I didn't take a salary for five and a half years, then paid myself $60,000 per year until 2020. I worked for ten years for basically nothing because I can tolerate a lot of risk. Originally, I gave myself two years, or until I ran out of money. I started the company with $49,000 of my personal money. I switched from coffee to tea because I could get Lipton tea bags for six cents apiece instead of $1 a cup when you make it at home. Everything was about conserving every penny. I almost ran out of money a bunch of times and got down to $411 in my bank account the second year. I was testing the market because I didn't want to be one of those people who didn't start something I loved.[1]

In retrospect, as difficult as crossing the cash gap was for them, all our CEOs were glad they didn't have to resort to giving up equity (and control).

As a business leader you need to understand the seven drivers of operating cash flow (price, volume, cost of goods, overheads, receivables, inventory, and payables). Most CEOs and business owners focus on cutting their selling, general, and administrative costs, or the typical balance sheet strategies such as paying vendors later and trying to collect from customers faster. These strategies have only a limited impact on your working capital and cash position.

Although our BFGs worked on cutting costs in all of these areas, pricing authority was the number-one factor that enabled them to fund their growth. I don't believe any of them strategically decided to be the premium price leader in their markets, but most generally were.

For instance, how did Farmgirl Flowers grow to $100 million in annual revenue in a few short years? Check out their prices! They are a high-end online floral provider creating a unique experience and product offering that supports their market position. This issue was particularly important for Farmgirl Flowers, as Son Pham, the former CFO of Farmgirl Flowers, explained to me:

> In the flower business, the first half of the year pays for second half. It's not abnormal to lose money for that period. But if you lose too much money, you're fighting for that oxygen—that cash supply. I tell Christina that if you don't find opportunities to increase your margin, you're in this vicious cycle where you're kind of paralyzed. You don't have money to invest. So it's a very unique situation where you have to be very creative and determined to get yourself out of that vicious cycle.[2]

When I made competitive comparisons for our BFGs, virtually none tried to compete on price; nor were they the lost-cost leaders. Most business owners intuitively understand that being the low-cost leader is a game of greater scale, so it's not a solid strategy when trying to scale faster. Creating a differentiated offering (which I cover in Chapter 6) allows you to raise your prices and is the number-one strategy you can execute to improve cash flow. Farmgirl Flowers does this exceptionally well; Son Pham described their position to me:

> So relative to everybody else, we would expect our products to be priced at a premium because of the design factor. If you put our products side by side with our competitors, hopefully, the customers out there would be able to identify our products because they're aesthetically better. Our products look much better than our competitors', and we believe that consumers are willing to pay a premium over our competitors' products.

Generating even greater sales volumes consumes more cash, so additional profitability generated through higher prices increases cash flow by 300 percent. There is no other lever you can pull that generates extra cash (and profits) faster and more directly than raising your price. PE investors understand this all too well, and it's generally one of the first places they look when they acquire a company.

Even billionaire investor Warren Buffett thinks this is the right focus. He says pricing power is the most important thing to him when evaluating a business.[3] Pricing power (or authority) comes back to having a strongly differentiated brand because, without that, a company wouldn't have the ability to raise prices easily in the long term. So, if you want to grow and scale faster and bootstrap that growth, look no further than providing a more valuable offer to your customers and raising your prices to reflect it.

> Check out our Book Resources section at www.scaleupfaster.com/resources to see how you can use better competitive positioning to create a differentiated offer to create pricing authority.

Chapter 12

LEVERAGE

KEY INSIGHTS

- Use machine learning and AI to improve cash flow management.
- Use simple cash flow simulations to forecast capital needs better.
- Leverage external capital sources to provide room to scale.

Use Artificial Intelligence to Improve Cash Flow Management

Accurate cash flow predictions enable businesses to make informed decisions about when to invest in growth initiatives and when to conserve cash. Emerging technologies, including AI and machine learning, can analyze patterns in a business's cash flow to predict future trends accurately and significantly improve cash flow management in businesses. By leveraging data analysis, predictive analytics, and automation, these technologies can enhance decision-making, forecast future cash flow with higher accuracy, and optimize operations. Here's how machine learning and AI can help improve cash flow:

- Predictive analytics for forecasting: machine learning models can analyze historical financial data to predict future cash flow trends, allowing businesses to anticipate periods of cash surplus or shortage.
- Automated invoice processing: AI can automate invoicing and accounts receivable, reducing the time it takes to process payments and improving the speed at which cash enters the business.
- Credit risk assessment: AI models can assess customers' creditworthiness more accurately by analyzing vast amounts of data, including credit history, transaction data, and market trends. A few of our BFGs are experimenting with this functionality and asked us not to identify them for competitive reasons.
- Optimized payment terms: AI can analyze payment histories and market conditions to suggest optimal payment terms for customers and suppliers.
- Expense management: By analyzing expenditure patterns, AI can identify areas where costs can be reduced without affecting business operations.
- Inventory management: AI can optimize inventory levels by predicting demand more accurately, ensuring that capital is not tied up unnecessarily in stock.
- Dynamic pricing models: AI can adjust pricing in real-time based on demand, competition, and market conditions to maximize revenue and improve cash flow.
- Fraud detection: AI and machine learning can detect unusual patterns that may indicate fraud or financial discrepancies early on. Banks and credit card companies have been using these technologies forever, but they are now accessible to virtually every business.

- Automation of financial operations: Beyond invoicing, AI can automate other financial operations like payroll, tax filing, and compliance reporting, reducing administrative costs and errors and freeing up cash that might otherwise be held in reserve to cover potential mistakes.

Implementing these technologies requires an initial investment and a period of adjustment. The long-term benefits include more accurate cash flow forecasting, improved decision-making capabilities, and enhanced operational efficiency, all of which contribute to better financial health and enable faster growth for your business.

Check out our Book Resources section at www.scaleupfaster.com/resources to see how you can use our AI-based platform to improve your operating cash flow by up to 35 percent.

Use Simple Cash Flow Simulation to Forecast Capital Needs Better

Using tools to simulate the impact of cash flow on various business decisions can help you understand where to focus your efforts and where you may need to focus on alternative funding sources. This goes beyond the cash flow forecasting tools available in most accounting packages and lets you easily simulate various scenarios that could affect cash needs.

For instance, how much cash would you need to increase your sales by 50 percent, 100 percent, or 200 percent? What would happen if you decided to raise your prices by 15 percent—you might lose a few customers (sales volume declines or growth slows), but perhaps you would make more money in the long run and generate more cash. The same goes for simulating reducing inventory, reducing cycle time, extending terms with suppliers, paying off loans faster, and collecting from customers faster. By looking at the company's previous income statement and balance sheets and then forecasting your capital requirements using various scenarios, you can take more control of your company's future.

> Check out the Resources section at www.scaleupfaster.com/resources for an example of our "Power of One" report, which shows how you can increase your company's operating cash flow by up to 30 percent by understanding the 1 percent or one-day changes in your seven key drivers and how you can use our tools to simulate the cash needs as you grow and scale.

Leverage External Capital Sources to Provide Room to Scale

A banker is a fellow who lends you his umbrella when the sun is shining but wants it back the minute it begins to rain.
—ATTRIBUTED TO MARK TWAIN

I mean no disrespect to my banker friends, but this quote is completely accurate (been there, done that, several times!). The relevance of this quote is evidenced by the fact that most BFGs could not get loans or lines of credit until they didn't need them anymore. Some CEOs just assumed this would be the case, so they didn't even try to secure financing, but many submitted applications and were denied. As discussed earlier in the book, most of them never had business plans until they were required to put one together for a bank.

Nevertheless, various external sources of capital did play a meaningful role in accelerating their growth. Many of the firms hit a threshold of growth (remember, on average, doubling revenues every year) where, even though they were generating enough cash to fund their growth, they wanted the safety net of a line of credit they could tap into if they needed it or wanted to make strategic acquisitions or investments. Today, alternative and non-traditional sources of capital to fund your growth are more available than ever, but optimizing your cash flow is still essential to securing the best terms (interest, covenants, personal guarantees, etc.). Simon Elsbury described their method of funding:

> Everything [our growth] was funded by the banks. We did all this stuff off something called an invoice discounting line. You just leverage a revolving loan off the most liquid asset that you've got on your balance sheet, and you can get a fairly decent interest rate just because it's low risk.

Chapter 13

REINVEST

Having the right rainy day fund to help cover shortfalls can be the difference between making it through some hard times and finding your business on life support. However, squirreling away too much cash can mean anemic growth and missed opportunities.

—BRUCE ECKFELDT, "CALCULATING YOUR BUSINESS'S RAINY DAY FUND IS NOT HARD IF YOU FOLLOW THESE STEPS"

KEY INSIGHT

- Continue to reinvest in your growth and enterprise value.

Even though many of the BFGs now have more than sufficient cash balances to fund future growth, they remain lean and cash-efficient in an effort to control their destinies. Virtually no one I spoke to pulled the cash out to fund the owner's lifestyle. Almost every leader is committed to keeping the business well-funded and in a position to take advantage of market opportunities. A few made small acquisitions, but the majority doubled down on expanding their market share as they felt they had just scratched the surface of their markets.

I asked whether they felt they had hit their stride, but none felt they had. Around half of the firms I spoke with that had revenues above $25 million mentioned that they were in a sufficient cash position to think more strategically about capital allocation and enterprise value.

A few firms who asked not to be identified made measuring their enterprise value the most important ownership metric even though they did not intend to sell their firm in the short term. My friend, John Warrilow, author of *Built to Sell*, would wholeheartedly agree with this approach. He thinks the owner's metric is the most important KPI to track (he thinks of it as the North Star metric) and believes it should inform strategic decisions made by the founder or owner. Although the rate of growth (especially compared to industry growth rates) is an essential factor in the valuation of a company, there are eight other factors you can work on as an owner to improve your company's value.

1. Financial performance: This refers to the historical revenue and profit numbers that demonstrate your company's ability to generate income and manage expenses effectively. Everything else being equal, better-than-industry-average gross and net margins will result in a higher valuation.
2. Growth potential: (That's why I wrote this book!) This is what we call scalability factor X (SFX). It is the future growth potential for your business to expand and increase its profitability by entering new markets, launching new products, or scaling operations. A higher SFX will result in a better valuation. The buyer needs to get a return on their investment from buying your company, and most of the time, this is where they will achieve their ROI.

3. Revenue and supply chain diversity: This is what we refer to as de-risking the business. The buyer will assess the risk associated with your dependence on any single customer, employee, or supplier. Diversification of any one of these items (especially revenue) reduces the risk associated with overreliance on any one entity.
4. Operating cash flow: A buyer will evaluate the predictability of your cash flows and the need for additional working capital. Businesses with more predictable streams of cash and positive operating cash flow—and consequently less need for working capital—are typically more valuable. Our Cash Flow Finder can help you improve your operating cash flow by up to 30 percent.
5. Recurring revenue: This is the extent to which the business has predictable and stable income streams that are expected to continue in the future, such as subscriptions or long-term contracts. This is what we call a consistent and predictable business.
6. Pricing authority: This is the uniqueness of the business and its products or services, which sets it apart from competitors and allows it to command higher prices and customer loyalty. This is what we call power product positioning, which can help maintain above-average margins and thus a higher valuation.
7. Customer satisfaction: This is an objective and evidence-based assessment of the level of satisfaction and loyalty among the business's customers, which can lead to repeat business, referrals, and a strong brand reputation. (This is not simply saying our customers are happy—have you ever heard an owner say anything different?) Beyond the assets and intellectual property, this is what a buyer is paying for; therefore, higher customer retention and opportunities for selling additional products and services is a primary purchase consideration for a buyer.

8. Team-managed company: This is the extent to which the business can operate independently of its owner. A business that can run smoothly without the constant involvement of the owner is typically more attractive to potential buyers and will keep you from agreeing to long-term performance-based earn outs.

These drivers are designed to help business owners increase the value of their companies, making them more appealing to potential buyers or investors.

> Check out our Resources section at www.scaleupfaster.com/resources to download a copy of the ebook *Owner's Metric: The One Number You Need to Truly Be Free.*

PART IV

Strategic Execution

strategize →
enhance →
outsource →
automate →
scale

Imagine the operational impact from doubling your company's revenues every year like the BFGs did. This level of growth and scale affects virtually everything in the business.

I specifically call this part "Strategic Execution" because I firmly believe that leaders must make the right short- and long-term decisions *and* effectively execute. Good strategy with poor execution is fruitless at best and disruptive at worst. Conversely, poor strategy executed well can send your company into a wall. You must get both right, or at least continue to test and experiment until you operationally nail the outcomes you are seeking.

The many decisions business leaders need to make run the gamut from strategic long-term decisions to very tactical decisions—what moves should you make tomorrow, and what should you focus on. There are countless decision frameworks to help you make better decisions, such as effort-impact analysis, SWOT analysis, cost-benefit, pros and cons, and more sophisticated ones like RICE, MoSCoW (look it up—this a great one), and others. (We use the Ansoff Matrix with our clients to evaluate growth strategies based on market and product dimensions.) I was interested in how our BFGs made these decisions, in what order, and how they ensured effective execution of the decisions they made.

What I learned from my research is that these companies were in constant states of reinvention and they had to figure it out as they went. I created the chapters in this part to reflect the operational maturity I witnessed from most of the firms.

Most of the BFGs started by continually enhancing their operational procedures without investing much money in automating systems. When they did invest, they usually invested in point solutions bought on the cheap.

As they scaled, they made decisions about what to outsource based on where they thought they had internal competency and capacity. Finance and bookkeeping were the most outsourced functions.

Once their businesses got more complex, they were forced to begin automating many of their operations with more sophisticated systems. In some cases, they built internal proprietary systems in an effort to keep from letting too many things fall through the cracks.

Finally, they got to the point where investing in enterprise-class systems and processes slightly ahead of their growth allowed them to truly scale. It was at this stage that profitability increased dramatically, and the flywheel effect took over.

Chapter 14

STRATEGIZE

The best strategy in the world is useless unless it's executed.

—ATTRIBUTED TO HOWARD SCHULTZ (FORMER CEO OF STARBUCKS)

KEY INSIGHTS

- Ditch the business plan.
- Create your own luck.
- Don't focus on your competitors.
- Forget the BHAG.

In line with Howard Schultz's statement at the start of this chapter, I want to distinguish between creating a solid strategy and successfully executing it. This is important to understand because a bad strategy executed well can run you off the cliff, and a good strategy with poor execution leaves you weak and vulnerable, sputtering from the starting line.

This chapter focuses on both concepts—what our BFGs thought about strategy and strategic planning and how they approach execution.

How do you create the right strategy and then execute it with precision?

Harvard Business School defines business strategy as "the strategic initiatives a company pursues to create value for the organization and its stakeholders and gain a competitive advantage in the market."[1] They suggest that strategy is crucial to a company's success and is needed before any goods or services are produced or delivered.

I guess many of the BFGs didn't listen to Harvard's advice, because they went out and started serving their customers *before* creating their strategy. Silicon Valley calls this "finding product market fit." None of our BFGs told me that's what they were doing when they started, but it's precisely what they were doing.

The BFGs I studied closely didn't have a real strategy, and virtually all of them were pretty sloppy on execution. I was quite surprised by how many of them, even with hundreds of millions of dollars of revenue, were still trying to figure this out. (I explain later why this is a good thing.)

Most of the BFGs fell into their strategy by testing, failing, falling down, getting back up, and then trying something else. For instance, David Freedman and his cofounder of Freestar had the "perfect strategy" to buy and flip e-commerce websites. They rebooted their strategy after burning through all the seed capital they had gotten from their friends and family. In David's words, they chased a lot of shiny objects, had a 50 percent customer churn rate, and blew through all their money. They hit restart with the same tech and a new business model and parlayed that into the BFG they are today. This has served them well, as they've built a culture of strategic flexibility and the will to try stuff without fear of failure.[2]

Don Wenner got his auspicious start as one of the top real estate agents in the country. He discovered through the evolution of his business that selling real estate wasn't a scalable model and that by transforming his business into a real estate development firm, he could have a much bigger company and impact. DLP took a while to find their core, but once they did, they stayed entirely focused on it and didn't easily waiver from it.[3]

Could developing your strategy be as simple as making decisions? Michael Sacca told me about Dribbble's focus on actions and decisions:

> There was way too much emphasis on "what if." . . . When we didn't make decisions, we got nothing done. We started to build a more entrepreneurial process where we were allowed to make mistakes. I think it's been one of the biggest cultural changes . . . having people say, "I'll take responsibility. Let's go in this direction." We can disagree and commit, but at least we're moving forward every day. It's simply asking the question is this reversible? Or is this not? And is this important? And is this not? Do I need to spend three days arguing, or can I just make this decision and move forward? And if I'm wrong, I'll fix it.[4]

This act of just making decisions unleashed Dribbble's growth. Too many leaders try too hard to create a long-term strategy they believe will bring the growth they desire instead of focusing on the market and needs of their customers—what we call "jobs to be done" in Part II. By staying close to your market and being flexible in your strategy, you'll naturally evolve into one that works for you and your team. Be open to allowing the market to take you in new directions; if you pay close enough attention, your customers will shape your strategy for you.

I want to clarify that I'm not suggesting that you'll grow faster by not having a strategy. But I will emphasize that spending all your time chasing the perfect strategy instead of the perfect customer will hinder your success.

Think of strategy as a GPS, but instead of a global positioning system, it is a growth positioning system. Like the GPS we use in our cars, boats, and planes, it's okay to go off track for a while and trust that eventually the GPS will bring you back on your path unless you decide on a new destination.

Ditch the Business Plan

Clarify your vision, and you will make better decisions about people, processes, finances, strategies, and customers.
—GINO WICKMAN, *Traction: Get a Grip on Your Business*

One of the questions I asked of all our BFGs was whether they had a business plan when they started. You know, the kind of fifteen-page, double-spaced perfect plan with a lot of beautiful charts and strong financial projections (which, of course, are completely made up).

Virtually none of the BFGs created a business plan when they started. The only two that did were started by founders with MBAs. (Well, of course, that's what they were taught to do when you start a company!) Kurt Donnell shares this mindset. He told me that he thinks "business plans are fairly useless at this point in time. You obviously have to put together some P&L to say can this thing make money and test the growth assumptions, but the sort of business school version of a business plan, I don't think so."[5]

Scott Andrew, who had started several companies before RSS, didn't have a formal business plan until three years into the company's life. "Of the businesses I started and scaled, the most successful was where we didn't create a business plan."[6] In my last company, we developed a manifesto that described the type of culture we wanted to build, the kinds of people we wanted to hire, and the types of customers we wanted to serve. There were no financials, long-term grand vision, or pages filled with content we made up for a banker, VC, or PE firm.

The BFGs told me that the first time they ever put together a proper business plan was when they needed one for acquiring a bank loan or line of credit. And when pressed about how well they executed that plan, most admitted that they rarely looked at it again. Zack Onisko, the former CEO of Dribbble, articulated this perspective on business plans when I interviewed him:

> I think with Eric Ries, Y Combinator and the new school approaches to building startups—they threw the idea of a business plan out the window. Instead, it was all about how you find product–market fit. And because 95 percent of startups fail, the faster you can find product–market fit, the faster there will be an actual business to invest in. That was the fuel on the kindling of the fire. From there you can throw oxygen on it, and it'll explode once you find that fit.[7]

I know that all bankers, VCs, PEs, business coaches, and academics are warming up their fingers to send me hate mail right now, but I can only report what I discovered. It even goes against my own schooling and gut instinct (I have an MBA, and I'm a planner). But during the two and a half years of my research, I began to understand that these founders, and subsequently their teams, birthed their businesses by listening to their markets. This makes complete sense to me, as the world is changing faster than ever. The founder and business leader who sit in their coworking space writing out a three-year business plan will quickly discover that the best-laid plans have a way of getting wrecked by the real world.

Now, I'm not suggesting you shouldn't plan. As Et Halstead, the COO for JCW Group, wisely says, "planning is essential; plans are useless."[8] He calls leading a company "hurdle racing," which is his theory that managing business growth is like constantly jumping over hurdles. You have an issue come up, you jump over it until another issue comes up, and you jump over that one—but you are consistently coming back round to fix new issues. Getting out of your office or house, talking to customers, and trying things trumps business planning every day. Christina Stembel also takes this approach:

> I'm a big fan of minimum viable product—get your MVP out there. I just showed somebody on my team who is a little perfectionist. For two and a half years, I had a picture on the front page of our website that was blurry. It wasn't even in focus. I just launched it and was like, whatever, I'm going to pretend that I wanted it to look a little fuzzy. Just get something out there because they're going to tell you whether they like it or not. I see people that have been working on a business idea for two years. I'm like, what the heck, get into it and you would have known a year and a half ago if this was a viable option.[9]

Make sure your plan and planning process is focused on understanding your customers better than your competitors. Do this first, and your strategy and how to execute it will naturally emerge. I know this sounds uncomfortable to most entrepreneurs, but it's far easier than having to figure everything out in advance.

> If not having a plan makes you completely nuts, check out our Resources section at www.scaleupfaster.com/resources for a strategic planning tool that will help you refine your growth plans; eliminate high-risk, low-probability options; and help you stop chasing shiny new objects.

Create Your Own Luck

At this point, you probably think these BFGs had no real strategy or business plan and most likely had no idea what they were doing. So, clearly, they got lucky.

You would be a little bit right.

In the book *Great by Choice*, written by Jim Collins and Morten Hansen, the authors developed the notion of return on luck. Collins and Hansen describe how, through their extensive research, some of the most significant companies of our time had a higher return on luck. They explain how these companies were not luckier than the others, but they could take better advantage of their luck than the comparison companies. To be sure, through all their research, they never found a single instance of sustained performance that was due to pure luck. But they never found a single great company devoid of lucky events along its journey.[10]

I generally don't believe in luck, but I do believe in serendipity (one of my favorite words and concepts), which I define as the intersection of opportunity and preparation. We come across opportunities every day, but we might not be prepared to notice or take advantage of them based on our degree of preparation.

Because our BFGs had such extraordinary success growing faster than most other companies, I wondered how luck played into their good fortunes. I asked each CEO whether they got lucky by having industry trends or world events lean in their direction. Christina Stembel acknowledged that some of their business decisions had turned out to have luck on their side:

> Until 2020, we always had big growth numbers. We never had to generate demand, but now I'm sitting in a different place completely from that. I didn't realize how lucky we were, and I don't use the word *lucky* ever. But it was pure luck that we started digital marketing when we did before the big companies understood that they should change their traditional marketing channels into digital ones.

Most of the CEOs I spoke with believed they were very fortunate (some said lucky) to have made the right strategic moves at the right time. This included COVID-19—all the companies I spent time with *grew* through COVID-19 because they changed course to take advantage of market opportunities or the acceleration to a more digital economy favored their business. Jamie Woods, the CEO of JCW Group, shared his thoughts on this topic with me and noted that his thinking has evolved over time:

> If you'd have interviewed me five to ten years ago, I would have told you there's no luck at all. It's all hard work and genius, etc. I wouldn't use the word genius now. I think there's a little luck in everything. I think any successful businessperson who says luck played no part in their success is slightly naive. You know, there's luck from day one of being born in a first-world country to good parents, etc. But if I look at the specifics of the business journey, almost every year there's been

> serendipitous things that you can trace back through your career; like what if that had happened slightly differently, or if I hadn't just made that decision at that particular time, then things could have turned out substantially differently.[11]

For example, OneScreen makes large interactive touch-screen panels for educators, and business nearly tanked during COVID-19 when schools shut down. But within months, the CEO began sourcing and selling temperature sensors for entrances to businesses and healthcare institutions. They recorded their best year ever in 2020 and created whole new customer segments and distribution partners.

The founder of Farmgirl Flowers, Christina Stembel, happened to be married to an executive from Facebook who convinced her to try advertising through their platform. This was well before her competitors were doing so, and it enabled the company's meteoric rise to well over $100 million in annual revenue in a very short period. Christina admitted that if she hadn't been married to him, she probably wouldn't have gone the route of social selling as their primary source of revenue.

Even Charlie Munger, the late great consigliere to Warren Buffet and one of the greatest investors in history, said that success solely from brilliance and hard work was nonsense. Charlie stated, "The records of people and companies that are outliers are always a reasonable amount of intelligence, hard work and a lot of luck."[12]

Another BFG that made its own luck is RIVA Solutions. CEO and founder Naveen Krishnamurthy created his luck by playing the odds. As a federal systems contractor, he didn't pursue the same large contracts everyone else was pursuing. He pursued projects that fewer companies competed for. Just like trying to get lucky gambling in Vegas, you improve your return on luck by playing the game with the best odds of winning. He described his thinking to me:

> I like probabilities. I think you can create your own luck by having your strategy play to your benefit of probability. Therefore, if you have enough deals in play where you have a 30 percent chance of winning, statistically, you're going to win. But I think a lot of people are like, no, I'm just going to chase the money and I'm now bidding against something where fifty other bidders are bidding. I don't want to bid like that. I want to bid on the thing where there's five bidders and then go for it. I think that definitely gave us a bit of an edge.[13]

Don't Focus on Your Competitors

What are we deeply passionate about? What can we be the best in the world at? What drives our economic/resource engine?
—**JIM COLLINS**, ***Good to Great***

In my interviews with the BFG CEOs, one conversation stuck out. It stuck out because of the story about how he viewed his competition. When Kyle Mitnick began learning about his direct competitors (affiliate marketing agencies), he discovered that their biggest competitors had an average of thirty clients. He was incredulous that they were proud of this (*"That's it?"* he emphatically asked). Kyle thought it was ridiculous that his industry had this tight-knit community, an old boys' club, with little to no new thinking. The last thing he wanted to do was to be like the competition.[14]

This passion for charting his own path has resulted in a client base that exceeds one thousand because he never focused on beating his competitors—he focused his company on serving his customers better than the entire industry.

For instance, one of the levers they pulled was to question the agency's practice of having account managers who tend to control relationships and information. Carlos Chilin, Advertise Purple's COO, told me, "Instead of an account manager stretched doing seven types of things, now we have departments filling each of those roles. Each department can become a specialist in that function and is, therefore, better than that person (account manager). This has allowed for much faster growth."[15]

Ruston Hughes, communications manager for Odyssey Engineering Group, stated that they consciously didn't follow the script of their large competitors. They didn't mimic what other successful engineering companies looked like; they structured their company to fit their vision. They did not copy the competitors' organizational structure or the way they went to market; they took their own path. They knew that the business would grow as fast as the culture would let it, and they let their culture differentiate it from its competitors.[16]

Retail Service Systems' BoxDrop franchise, which sells sofas and mattresses, doesn't fear what many other businesses fear—the Amazon effect. They created a business model nearly immune to what Amazon and the large digital firms can do: They let you see, touch, and sit on a sofa before you buy it, and then you can take it home immediately. Unlike the big furniture retailers that show the merchandise but rarely deliver same-day sofas, they only carry a few models to reduce inventory costs so that you can take them home with you (which is what most customers prefer). Charting their own path has led to impressive and continuous growth.

Forget the BHAG?

With all due respect to Jim Collins and Jerry Porras, who coined the term Big Hairy Audacious Goal (BHAG) in their book *Built to Last*, and to my friend and partner, Verne Harnish, who promotes it in his work with fast-growth companies and his book *Scaling Up*, the BHAG is not working for most of our BFGs. Admittedly, I'm not sure why. BHAG refers to a clear and compelling lofty target an organization tries to reach. Typically, it is a target that defines the company's mission and ignites every team member's passion to do everything they can to reach it.

Just like most of our BFGs didn't create a business plan or strategic roadmap, very few of our BFGs set a BHAG for their companies. I asked many of the CEOs and their leadership teams questions about how important it was to have everyone coming together to achieve some bold mission they had set out to accomplish. In other words, what was the company's BHAG?

What I heard was crickets.

To be fair, the concept of a mission did play a role in a few of the companies I interviewed and a few dozen more that I studied but didn't directly interview, but for the most part, this seemed to be missing with most of the BFGs. And it's not like these are small companies that haven't yet broken out—many have grown to hundreds of millions of dollars in revenue.

I wondered whether there was any difference between BHAGs that focused on making their customers' lives measurably better versus BHAGs that focused on taking over a market or industry. Clearly, Elon Musk and his companies have transformed several industries. In Ashlee Vance's biography, *Elon Musk: Tesla, SpaceX, and the Quest for a Fantastic Future*, she writes that Musk's BHAG is "to enable human exploration and settlement of Mars."[17] Based on my interviews with our BFGs, I have to wonder whether his team at SpaceX is driven by the goal to get to Mars or by the intellectual curiosity of figuring out how to do that. In other words, do they *really* want to send someone to Mars, or is it intellectually challenging to see whether they can do it?

We're taught in business (by Jim, Verne, Gino, and many others) to set huge, almost unreachable goals. If you dream of building a billion-dollar company or finding a cure for cancer, start with a grand goal and work backward from there. We're taught to break these big goals into smaller steps, make a plan for today, and constantly adjust it to stay on the right path. This approach is said to give us focus and motivation.

However, recent studies (including my study of our BFGs) tell a different story. The research suggests that setting ambitious goals can sometimes be more of a hurdle than a help, especially with regard to significant achievements and innovations. Surprisingly, goals might even drain our motivation instead of boosting it.

Goals can cause us to overlook unexpected opportunities (a phenomenon observed by researcher Richard Wiseman). They can leave us feeling empty once achieved and become outdated as the world changes.

What's the alternative to this BHAG-focused model? It's effectively what our BFGs have unknowingly done. It's called the stepping-stone approach (which is precisely how Musk approaches problems), in which success comes from following interesting and novel paths that might not seem directly related to your ultimate aim. This method is more about exploration and discovery than just ticking off milestones.

In their work on artificial intelligence, Kenneth Stanley and Joel Lehman argue that this approach is more effective for complex, real-world problems.[18] Instead of strictly following a set goal, you look for what's new and exciting and let that guide you to your next step.

This idea might sound unconventional, but it's backed by evidence. It suggests that true greatness and innovation might come from having no fixed objective but constantly seeking out what's new and exciting. Scott Andrew shared their version of this concept with me:

> As a rule, if you haven't made three or four mistakes throughout the year, you're really not trying. We've always got projects that we call swinging for the fences and those that fall under our R&D expenses. And sometimes we hit home runs, and sometimes they're complete strikeouts, but we're in to play all the time.

The CEO of Freestar, Kurt Donnell, explained the way they implement this concept:

> I'm a big believer in trying to be the best at one thing you can be the best at. Once you've done that, go one swim lane over, but don't try to boil the ocean, chase the shiny objects, and do all those things. If somebody else has built a company around something, that'd be a feature for you. It's probably better to partner with them and let them build that thing. Stick to the knitting—go do the thing that you're great at.

Not having a BHAG didn't make our BFGs aimless (nor should it deter you if you don't have one). They all had a general strategic direction, adjusted their strategy as the real world threw them curveballs, and focused on their customers' needs and what they could operationally execute. Rather than working backward from a stubbornly held goal, they took steps in that general direction and kept repeating, sensing, and stepping forward (sometimes even stepping backward or sideways).

One major exception to developing a BHAG with cascading goals is DLP Capital. In my interviews with people at DLP, they mentioned that their strategy document really served as their guiding light. Their strategy is shared with the entire company and lays out where they want to be in one year, three years, five years, and even ten years from now. And it includes all the key financial metrics they need to hit to achieve those goals.

If foregoing BHAGs and other goals doesn't sit well with you, or if setting them helps get you up in the morning and motivates you and your team, then set them. But I know plenty of people and companies that don't seem to have lofty stated goals but are incredibly successful anyway. It's easy to get caught up in conventional wisdom and what everyone else is doing, but as I've seen, most of our BFGs have carved their own paths. In fact, a few of our BFGs set lofty growth goals but backed off because they felt that they were pursuing growth for the sake of growth and not fulfilling either internal or external needs.

Remember, the path to real innovation and achievement might lie in a more open-ended and curiosity-driven approach. Therefore, the next time you contemplate your BHAG and goal setting, leave room for exploration and serendipity—it might lead you to your greatest successes.

Chapter 15

ENHANCE

Watch the little things; a small leak will sink a great ship.

—ATTRIBUTED TO BENJAMIN FRANKLIN

KEY INSIGHTS

- Eliminate inefficiencies that affect customers.
- Push down development of SOPs to where work is done.
- Create a decision framework and push down decision-making.
- Implement best of breed small and medium business systems before you scale up.

When leading a company, there is generally no shortage of fires to put out, decisions to be made, people to manage, clients to please, and suppliers to deal with. So how does one tackle the ever-growing need for your attention? That's what I am going to help you with in this chapter. I mention in an earlier chapter that I was surprised by the level of operational messiness of our BFGs. But as I look back at my career selling enterprise resource planning systems like SAP and Microsoft Dynamics, I shouldn't have been surprised because I have come to recognize that all businesses are messy. Since companies are a collection of messy humans constantly evolving and growing, naturally they are too.

I have sold process automation software for most of my professional career, so I can easily see whether a company is running like a well-oiled machine or is trying to fix the engine of a speeding car with chewing gum and paper clips.

As disconcerting as it is, trying to fix the engine with chewing gum speeding down the raceway is the natural state of growing and scaling! Each growth phase requires new processes, people, operational challenges, and levels of complexity, so, of course, every growth story is a work in progress. This is rarely a one-time set and forget endeavor. As the business grows and customer needs change, you'll find new areas for improvement and ways to become more efficient.

I found many common themes in how our BFGs met these challenges during each phase of their growth from start-up to maturity. I highlight DLP capital as my star process-efficient case study. Their dedication to becoming the most productive company in the world has paid off in straight-line growth for the past ten years into a business with multiple billions in assets under management.

I finish this part of the book with a deeper analysis of how DLP has pulled off this amazing operational efficiency. In the next few chapters, I detail how you can manage your own chaos as you grow faster and scale up your company.

Eliminate Inefficiencies That Affect Customers

DLP Capital has turned a quest toward efficiency and productivity into a strategic competitive advantage. That's the main point I want to get across here. You can focus on many facets of a business—accounting, finance, sales, supply chain—but the most essential processes to focus on are those that add value to the customer. One of our BFGs, whose name I won't disclose to protect the guilty, literally ran their back-office accounting on Google Sheets until they approached $100 million in annual revenue! I was blown away to learn that their accounts payable and receivables were kept on a Google sheet and reviewed weekly by the CEO. But they had incredible customer service, and their customers loved the company and their products (they still do). They focused on the customer experience, not their back office.

Back to DLP. DLP serves the property development industry where loans for large, complex projects can take anywhere from six weeks to several months to secure. The interest rate differentials aren't wide between lenders, so the ability to close a loan becomes a key differentiator in winning projects. DLP removed all of the friction, but not the risk, of funding projects. They are fast. They are able to close on loans within two or three weeks instead of the two or three months it takes their competitors. That has been a huge factor in their ability to gain market share.

Whether you implement a formal Kaizen type of program internally, you need to foster a culture of continuous improvement. Processes that directly affect (or are affected by) productivity and capital preservation can become a forcing function for you and your team to continue to improve your operations. Key measures such as revenue or profit per employee are great metrics to drive more efficiency as you scale.

I mention in the "Team" part of this book that our BFGs were good at strategically considering whether they needed that additional person before they submitted the job posting. This is the opposite of most VC-backed companies, which seem to compete to hire the most people, whether they need them or not. Mark Hodges, design and plan production group manager at Odyssey Engineering Group, described how they deal with this issue when I interviewed him:

> Everybody's trying to hire more people. Trying to find good people was only getting more difficult, so it wasn't like we could throw more resources at the problem. We had to be more efficient with our resources to take on more work. We've added a lot of incremental steps along the way to ensure that we're staying on track and not veering off course because it's bound to happen. There's a lot less course correction whenever we take these steps. We're adding steps, but it's not necessarily adding work. It's adding communication to the process.[1]

Create Standard Operating Procedures Where Work Is Done

Companies that grow and scale faster focus on the super boring but incredibly important area of SOPs. Developing SOPs in your business provides many benefits, including removing bottlenecks, improving process flow, training new employees, and ensuring quality and consistency. And even though so many business leaders intellectually understand this, in my experience, very few actually do anything about it. Keep these points in mind as you think about your business:

- SOPs are the foundations of building a thriving business while giving the founder the freedom to work when and where they want. It is even more critical if you want to support a remote team.
- SOPs help you to provide your customers with a consistent experience.
- SOPs allow you to preempt most questions your employees will have so they don't come to you with problems.

- SOPs give your people clear instructions for mastering the main tasks that make up their jobs.
- If you ever want to sell your company, SOPs give an acquirer confidence that your business will continue to succeed after you leave. Companies that can sustain a three-month absence of the owner are more than twice as likely to receive a premium offer.

Have your employees create SOPs for their most important tasks so that anyone can take them over when they are out of the office. I know this can be a difficult sell because they might feel that it makes them more susceptible to being laid off. As part of this effort, ask them to identify which tasks they work on that can be eliminated, automated, or potentially outsourced to free them up to do higher-level tasks. Create a list of tasks they perform and let them know they are the owner of their function and will oversee any tasks (and the results) that are part of their responsibilities. Brill Media has done this, as Linda Monsour told me: "We've implemented a set of processes and systems that will set the client's campaigns up for success."[2]

Special note: Top performers will not challenge the idea of creating SOPs because they want to grow beyond their position. Individuals who fight to document and improve what they do every day do this out of fear of losing their job or being replaced, so ensure that by doing this, you are relieving stress points for them and allowing them to do better and more efficient work.

One of the difficulties of creating solid SOPs is that processes, especially in start-ups, are continually changing. But the process of creating the SOPs helps ensure that all team members are aligned around the company's mission, and quality SOPs help people figure out the best paths around obstacles.

I like how Et Halstead describes SOPs (and the metrics for measuring the business) as his guidance and control systems. Everyone knows how safe flying is relative to any other means of transportation. Imagine if the pilots and crew made it up each time they were ready to take off.

That's what so many companies do. But not our beloved BFGs. They have the discipline and leadership to refine, document, and improve their processes, which is fundamental to handling a doubling of the business every year, as most of them have done. This is not to suggest that putting in place SOPs will ensure you can grow faster, but I know that not doing so will stifle your long-term growth. Et reinforced this point and talked about the enormous benefits they reaped from creating SOPs when I interviewed him:

> In actual fact, you can do the same sales process almost anywhere in the world. And doing so meant that we could streamline training so that everyone knew the same terminology. Everyone was operating the same way. Everyone was moving together as a unit. And the systems enabled us to create the guidance system for that. It's a system that guides itself, but also the control to prevent people going off base. You end up with this kind of guidance and control system that gives people everything they need to focus on what they should be doing.

Check out our Resources section at www.scaleupfaster.com/resources to download a copy of our *Definitive Guide to Standard Operating Procedures*.

Create a Decision Framework and Push Down Decision-Making

Decision-making can hinder your rate of growth. My friend and partner, John Warrilow, discusses the hub and spoke decision-making system, where virtually every decision must go through the CEO: "Imagine Chicago O'Hare or Heathrow, which act as centralized routing locations for the airlines that rely on them. The system works efficiently enough until a snowstorm shuts down a hub, and then the entire transportation system grinds to a halt." That could be your company!

Imagine you're the hub and you run your business with every essential issue coming through you. It's efficient until you are no longer there to run things, so anyone valuing your business will levy a steep discount, and your growth will be stifled.

Here are some telltale signs to help you know if you are the hub, which can stunt your growth:

1. You are responsible for signing all the checks. What would happen if you were away for a few days and an important supplier needed to be paid?
2. Your revenue is the same as last year's, which might indicate that your business operates like a hub in a hub-and-spoke model with you as the primary constraint to new sales.
3. You find yourself spending more time negotiating everything—approving discounts for customers, terms with suppliers, and so on.
4. You are the only person who knows how to close up your business at the end of the day, including counting the cash, locking the doors, and setting the alarm.
5. You know all of your customers by their first names. If you know every single customer personally, it might indicate that your business relies too much on your direct relationships, which are essential for keeping your business running.

Reducing your business's reliance on your everyday involvement frees up time for you to think about the company more strategically and invest more of your energy in business activities that fully leverage your unique skillset. When our BFG CEOs hit this transition point, they unleashed decision-making into the organization—and their growth accelerated. Zarrar Kahn, projects and logistics manager for OneScreen, told me what you should be focusing on inside of working *in* your business:

> You should spend a minimum of time using your keyboard. I should not see you typing. I should not see you working. I should see you thinking. That's the goal of operations. With the daily stuff you feel you need to do; it should happen without your need to participate. Essentially, your job should be to think, hey, okay, well, what else can we do better? How do we do that? But you can only do that when you have free time on your hands. I tell this to my team all the time.[3]

Chapter 16

OUTSOURCE

Do what you do best and outsource the rest.

—ATTRIBUTED TO PETER DRUCKER

KEY INSIGHTS

- Outsource back-office functions; retain customer-facing processes.
- Build a culture-fit external team.

Outsource Back-Office Functions; Retain Customer-Facing Processes

Our BFGs were all able to grow with internally generated cash, which I discuss in Part III. They were able to do this largely because they consistently and strategically outsourced functions at the right time along their growth curves. Part of their business strategy, consciously or not, was to outsource their back-office functions while insourcing most or many customer-facing activities.

Our BFGs understood that the customer experience is a significant differentiator, and they wanted to ensure that this responsibility was not abdicated to a third party. No BFG I interviewed outsourced any function that directly touched the customer. Many other companies can provide these customer-facing functions, so I asked the BFGs why they kept those tasks in house. Most of them stated that their in-house teams are more aligned with the company's culture and values, which they believe are crucial for maintaining a consistent customer experience.

Outsourcing the non-customer-facing functions gave them the cost-savings and flexibility to change vendors and systems as they grew. Imagine having to retool your accounting, finance, and HR systems every few years as you double your business annually. (That sounds awful!) This is better left to the experts. Many of our CEOs admitted that they wished they would have hired an internal expert finance person (CFO or vice president of accounting and finance) sooner than they had, but none believed it had held back their growth. Neelu Modali told me that they fluctuated between keeping back-office functions in house or outsourcing them, depending on where they were in their growth cycle:

> Remember those financial inflection points I was telling you about? As I approached those, it made sense to insource or outsource depending on whether you're at the bottom or the top of those ranges. . . . Now we're at a point where we brought it back in-house and now everything is in-house.[1]

Not unexpectedly, the most common functions and systems outsourced were accounting, finance, HR, and payroll. A few companies outsourced their entire people operations to a professional employer organization (PEO), which recruits and hires the team on your behalf and then leases them back to your company. Michael Chavira of Axiologic stated that using a PEO in their first few years was crucial for their rapid growth since they didn't have to worry about hiring, firing, benefits, or payroll and could focus on selling new projects. He told me that, "If I had to do it again, I would still hire a PEO because it would save a lot of headaches and time to get things set up."[2] At first, they were trying to do it all in house, including managing their own health care costs, but it was expensive. Using the PEO worked well for them and helped them manage these costs. Michael said that eventually they transitioned away from using the PEO:

> Now that I know a lot more about how PEOs operate, there are certain PEOs I'd work with and others I wouldn't. We found one that we liked, and we could grow with them. Then we got to a point of . . . let's put them on PEO light; let's start bringing in some of these functions. Over the next three or four years, we eliminated the use of the PEOs. But I would say this was one of the biggest inflection points.

Making outsourcing work for you isn't without its challenges. Integrating external and internal teams requires robust communication channels and a clear understanding of shared goals, as many of our BFGs have discovered. Michael Sacca told me about some of the communication challenges they had faced:

> We started to screen for communication because we realized that when we're remote, we need this no matter what the position is. We needed people who were highly versed in communicating and even overcommunicating. Because the biggest time suck is siloing. And

> people are kind of working in a bubble. It was happening all the time. We started to hire skilled people, but more importantly [people who] were good at and thrived on that level of extra communication.

Build a Culture-Fit External Team

As Kurt Donnell dubbed it, "remote by design" was the reigning employment method of our BFGs—working not only from home but also from across the globe. Farmgirl Flowers now gets their flowers from South America. Most companies like Dribbble, Brill Media, and Farmgirl Flowers launched and grew their companies this way, and some, like Freestar, moved in that direction after COVID-19.

Building a culture of communication and collaboration was a necessity for Freestar with its far-flung workforce, and it also inspired the notion that their company could hire a workforce from anywhere in the world. Freestar built a team in Bulgaria, which Kurt described to me:

> We previously had an office, our headquarters in Phoenix. And then we had offices in New York and LA. People hated it, particularly in LA, commuting and everything else. It's expensive to hire people in New York and LA. I was convinced we could hire some other people in other markets cheaper than New York and LA. I finally convinced David [the cofounder] to let me give it a shot. My first remote employee was great. So we built the ability to hire in lower-cost markets, or at least expand the talent pool to find people when we couldn't early on. As a result, we've built this remote-by-design business, versus the businesses that ended up

> remote by default in COVID-19. I think the ones that have struggled growing remotely or hybrid is because they were remote by default, where your culture was intended to be built in person, but then you kind of make it online. I think the decision we had made pushed us really hard to open the aperture to where we could hire people. We now have thirteen top people in Bulgaria, which has been fantastic.

Cultural fit is often overlooked in hiring external teams, yet it's crucial for long-term success. When integrating an external team from a different part of the world, getting them to understand and align with your organization's culture becomes a keystone for seamless collaboration. As outlined in Part I, our BFGs were very good at articulating their culture to potential full-time hires, which attracted culture-fit top performers to their companies. But the ones that decided to hire external teams from abroad frankly stumbled many times before they got it right. What made the difference in getting it right? They learned to apply the same cultural filter to their external teams as they did with their internal hires.

They knew that these external teams were an extension of their internal teams, regardless of their roles, and that creating alignment was critical; having shared values enabled this alignment. It doesn't mean there weren't cultural differences; of course there were. But identifying vendors, partners, and consultants who shared the same values, such as over-communication and accountability, was the primary factor in successfully extending their teams. Robert Brill told me about his recommendations for finding the right staff members:

> I would take massive advantage of the global workplace—people who are talented in Estonia and

> different parts of Eastern Europe, India, and the Philippines. I will take massive advantage of that labor force where possible. There are some pros and cons to that, but that's what I would do. If I were starting again from scratch, I'd be interested in keeping costs down as much as possible and this would help. Every dollar you save today gives you runway for tomorrow.[3]

Their internal teams' willingness to adjust to other cultures, time zones, and ways of working contributed to these successful relationships. In most cases, this was facilitated by treating the external team members as truly part of the team, and they were included in regular interactions beyond work. They shared photos of their personal lives and held virtual coffees, lunches, dinners, and cultural exchange sessions to build more personal connections.

As detailed in their book *Exponential Organizations 2.0: The New Playbook for 10× Growth and Impact*, Salim Ismail, Peter H. Diamandis, and Michael S. Malone note that using the world of talent to create staff-on-demand can help drive faster growth and profitability. They back this up with data that shows that the top ten companies in the Fortune 100 who used this strategy outstripped their counterparts in every key metric:

- 40 times higher shareholder returns
- 2.6 times better revenue growth
- 6.8 times higher profitability
- 11.7 times better return on assets turnover[4]

This proved to be so for the BFGs as well. Those who developed workforce flexibility and searched for talent anywhere in the world built the organizational muscle, cultural sensitivity, communication methods, and global mindset that allowed them to grow faster than their competitors. Integrating an external team from a different part of the world is not just about outsourcing work; it's about building bridges across cultures. When done right, it doesn't just add to your workforce; it enriches your organization's cultural tapestry, leading to a more diverse, inclusive, and innovative workplace.

Check out our Resources section at www.scaleupfaster.com/resources for our *Global Hiring Guide*, on how to hire teams across the globe more effectively.

Chapter 17

AUTOMATE

Automation enables people to focus
on tasks that require the human touch.

—ATTRIBUTED TO JACK MA

KEY INSIGHTS

- Follow this sequence: enhance → outsource → automate → scale.
- Implement systems and processes slightly in advance of your size and complexity.
- Decide whether to create your own best practices or follow others.

The Sequence

I lay out the beginning of Part IV this way—enhance → outsource → automate → scale—for a specific reason. Whether it was a forethoughtful way to grow faster or just happened by accident, this is the sequence of operational capability most of our BFGs took to bootstrap faster growth. I've been in the enterprise resource planning and process automation industry for twenty years, so to learn that these beloved companies weren't refining and automating their processes in the early days was like heresy to me—of course it's all about process, right?!

But after so many conversations, it all made sense to me. In just about all the cases, these companies evolved so much over their early years that to focus on building robust processes from the beginning was time, effort, and investment they didn't need to make—they needed to figure out who they were going to serve and how they were going to do it better than anyone else. Of course this was the proper focus.

But once they got to a specific size, refining their processes, figuring out what to outsource, and then automating what they could gave them the organizational infrastructure they needed to turn on the jets. I get into how they began to scale in the next chapter, but here, I want to highlight how and what they decided to automate.

The BFGs evaluated their internal capacity and capability to decide whether their current processes were capping their potential. They inherently knew that automating mundane tasks would free up their employees for more creative and strategic work, unleashing new growth (and boosting morale). A few of their operational leaders admitted that they undertook these efforts later than they should have, which caused operational inefficiency and maybe even leaky cash flow. Still, once they decided what to do, they went about setting the stage for even faster growth. Robbyn Jackson, vice president of operations at Mindpath College Health, shared their path with me:

> We got pretty far down the road without many systems or hardly any departments. But then we got too big, and then we had no infrastructure. With no systems in place, we started to turn our attention to the infrastructure of the company and the need to build it because there was this feeling like we were all living in a house of cards that would fall down any day. We had to pause our growth and focus on putting systems in place, paying for systems that we never thought we would need or how much they would cost. It actually halted our growth.[1]

For the BFGs, the decision of when to automate their internal systems was not taken lightly. It usually involved substantial financial and operational investment as they pulled people out of the business to work on the automation. They were growing fast, but not exponentially. They knew that teams were stretched thin, so the question with most of them wasn't whether they should automate, but when. It was a strategic choice at the intersection of internal readiness and competitive necessity.

This is a valuable lesson for all businesses trying to figure out how much they begin automating their operations, whether through implementing enterprise systems or otherwise. It's not just about the technology or the potential efficiencies. It's about understanding where you are in your growth cycle, assessing available internal and external skills, looking at the financial feasibility, and knowing when it's the right time to accelerate your growth.

Implement Systems and Processes Slightly in Advance of Your Size and Complexity

Bootstrapped growing businesses often face a paradox: the need to prepare for future growth while conserving cash and managing the present.

It's easy to sink gobs of money into systems, processes, and people ahead of the growth that's sure to come, only to confront the need to replace people and systems when the business changes or the growth never comes. The tricky balance is to invest in people and systems slightly ahead of the need. Our BFGs let the stress of people and processes get loud but not overwhelming before they made significant investments in hiring or acquiring new systems.

Back when people went into the office, this sounded like listening to the complaints of overcrowding for six to nine months (maybe even longer) before you addressed the problem. Our BFGs seemed to have a reasonably good second sense that helped them know when the time was right. When I had every CEO take me through inflection points in their growth, very few saw far enough ahead with the clarity to make the investments earlier. It became more of a function of hiring the professional water bailer to bail out the water before the boat sank. The CEOs had no regrets when I asked about the stress of letting operations get to that point before they pulled the trigger of investing in their operational capacity.

RIVA has doubled revenues every year for the past six years, and without paying at least some attention to scaling its infrastructure, this would have been nearly impossible. RIVA invested slightly ahead of what the business needed, even though they knew it was a strain on the company. It was a constant battle between getting ahead of the growth and conserving cash. When they did invest, they always bought systems slightly larger than they needed. Their COO, Neelu Modali, explained their thinking to me:

> I think the philosophy was, let's always buy bigger shoes. It's kind of like the dad who goes to the store and says, well, you're going to be a size eight next month anyway so let's buy size eight even though you are a size six

> and a half right now. We were constantly buying those size eights, whether it was office space, personnel, sales folks, systems, software, infrastructure, or whatever. We were going to build for when we were larger. We were not going to buy for now. And that was by design. And it was very, very stressful. It was very stressful financially. It was like the plane was trying to go Mach 12, and all the rivets and all the nuts and bolts were starting to pop off. Any time anybody asked me about running our business, I said I'm hanging out the window of the school bus and trying to put the tires and wheels on it. It's just bootstrapping constantly.

According to Mark Hodges, they would always hire slightly ahead of the need from both an individual contributor and a leader perspective. The engineering firm's ability to scale up depends on their ability to bring in talented engineers, and it can take six months to recruit and hire a top engineer, not to mention the time needed to onboard, train, and integrate them into the organization. I faced this same issue with my last consulting firm, and we were forced to identify the core skills that we would always be recruiting and hiring for, regardless of need, and other specialized skills we could find on a freelance basis. Bob Peterson, the CFO of DLP Capital stressed the importance of core values when I interviewed him:

> The Elite Execution System is really what we live by. And, I mean, it's not just core values that are on a table somewhere. I mean, those are lived and an integral part of our business. People who aren't aligned with that aren't really happy here, because the culture is pretty deep. And so the people who remain and are retained here are fully involved in the Elite Execution System.[2]

In this fast-paced business world, it's not just about how quickly you grow but how well-prepared you are to handle that growth. As companies scale, implementing systems and processes slightly in advance of their current needs is not just a strategy; it's a necessity for sustainable success.

Create Your Own Best Practices or Follow Others?

In the quest for faster business growth, a pivotal question often surfaces: Should companies create their own best practices or emulate the strategies of other successful companies? While the allure of proven methodologies is undeniable, the efficacy of pioneering unique practices cannot be overlooked.

And what are best practices exactly? Who defines what is best and decides what's a practice? Many vendors, especially software vendors, will tout that their software is based on best practices, but the truth is that it may or may not be best for you.

The concept of following established best practices is grounded in the notion of learning from the successes and failures of others. A strategy that propels a tech start-up to success may not yield the same results for a manufacturing firm. The 2021 McKinsey Quarterly emphasized that only 20 percent of best practices are universally applicable, with the remaining 80 percent requiring adaptation to specific industry and company contexts.[3]

Certainly, there are a lot of internal processes that are universal, and that you shouldn't invest any money or effort into, especially those concerning regulatory or compliance practices, including financial and government-mandated practices. But outside of that, you must decide what practices fit your company best.

There was virtually no consistency in the software platforms (which contained best practices) used by our BFGs to run and scale their businesses. They used various financial and accounting systems, including Xero (used by one of our $85 million in revenue BFGs), NetSuite, and QuickBooks, and various customer relationship management systems such as HubSpot, spreadsheets, Salesforce.com, and email marketing systems I've never heard of. They used niche manufacturing and supply chain platforms and industry-specific software packages. I expected to hear about some common business operating platforms like EOS,[4] Scaling Up, and others. A few BFGs used these, but generally, most companies charted their own path forward.

What lesson does this hold for business leaders trying to grow and scale faster? Should you pick off-the-shelf systems that embody best practices, or invest the time, money, and effort into developing your own? Trying to become a software or process development firm is typically not at the core of what most companies do, so choose an area of your business where you believe you have intellectual or process superiority and only focus on that domain—leave everything else to off-the-shelf platforms.

Our BFGs universally took a hybrid approach. They appeared to use the least expensive solutions for taking care of their essential needs (finance, payroll, HR, etc.) to keep back-office costs down, then invested the capital and effort into developing their own secret sauce, or they looked for very industry-specific systems that met their needs at the moment. Et Halstead told me how JCW Group approached this issue:

> We didn't have a preexisting notion of how things should be. All we had was a whole list of problems. And when I say a whole list of problems, I mean an extensive list of problems. I mean, we just knew everything that didn't work. They say failure is good, right? Failure isn't good; learning from failure is good. And that is what we do very well. So the first time we came to systemize

> things, we rejected the urge to follow out of the box—here's how you should do it. Instead, we looked at this list of problems and said, this is what we need to do. This is what we need to be thinking about. This is what we need to work with and how we need to do things.

Based on their rapid growth rates (doubling nearly every year), the BFGs instinctively knew that they would quickly outgrow their systems. It's like buying clothing for a teenager growing two inches or more per year—you learn that the clothes you just bought may only last a year.

Adopting established best practices and creating your own is not a binary decision. The most effective strategy lies in understanding the unique aspects of your business and blending the wisdom of proven practices with the courage to innovate. The key is not to choose one path over the other but to navigate the dynamic balance between the two. Take the processes that make you unique and competitive and that add value to the customer experience, and either find systems that make you better or develop your own, like Advertise Purple, JCW, Farmgirl Flowers, and others.

Check out our Resources section at www.scaleupfaster.com/resources to download our ebook *The Yes Box*, which shows you how to reinvigorate and expand your business by focusing on step change improvements.

Chapter 18

SCALE

Only those who will risk going too far
can possibly find out how far one can go.

—ATTRIBUTED TO T. S. ELIOT

KEY INSIGHTS

- Be like Amazon and act like it's Day One—fear hubris and continue to act like a bootstrapped company.
- Build a team-managed company.
- Begin to focus on your enterprise value.

Be Like Amazon and Act Like It's Day One

Finding a concept as enduring and influential as Amazon's Day One philosophy is rare. At its core, Day One is about never losing the hunger and humility of a start-up. Bezos wrote in his 1997 letter to shareholders, "This is Day 1 for the Internet and, if we execute well, for Amazon.com."[1] This statement wasn't just a declaration of intent but a manifesto for a culture that refuses to rest on its laurels. This principle encapsulates a mindset of perpetual innovation, agility, and a relentless focus on customer satisfaction.

Despite massive success for all our BFGs, they all fear hubris and strive to maintain a bootstrapped mindset. They seemed to exemplify the title of Intel CEO Andy Grove's book: *Only the Paranoid Survive.* Perhaps the path to their collective success was filled with so many mental and emotional scars that they feared they could slip into irrelevance, or worse. Many of the CEOs I spoke with who had revenues well into the hundreds of millions of dollars along with tens of millions of dollars sitting in their corporate bank accounts didn't seem to notice that they had made it. Sure, they stressed a little less from a financial perspective, but they didn't want to take their foot off the gas or jump off to an exit. Something inside seemed to drive them toward further success from a business and personal perspective. (I talk about this in the next chapter.) A few of our CEOs stepped back to chair their board and let others take the reins daily, but they were still very much involved.

They all consciously wanted to maintain their bootstrap mentality. None of the CEOs I spoke with pulled money out of the business, even though they could have pulled millions out to fund new lifestyles for themselves. They were focused on the greater goal of making an impact through their companies. They knew that staying lean and mean with capital reserves was part of their recipe for success, enabling greater outcomes for all of their stakeholders.

Check out our Resources section at www.scaleupfaster.com/resources for more information on Amazon's Day One philosophy and how to apply it to your company.

Build a Team-Managed Company

I asked the CEOs and their teams this question: How involved was the founder in running day-to-day operations, particularly with regard to nurturing customer relationships? I wanted to keep the founders and CEOs honest by asking their executives just in case they had misconceptions about how involved they were.

A key to growing faster and scaling is to develop a company that is truly run by the leadership team. This probably sounds like an obvious statement, but I've come across many fast-growth companies where the CEO was ready to burn out because she was running a thousand miles per hour trying to keep everything from crashing down even while being convinced that her team was running the show.

At its heart, running a team-managed company is about more than just delegating tasks. It's about fostering a culture of shared responsibility, mutual respect, and collective decision-making. A *Harvard Business Review* study revealed a staggering 40 percent increase in employee engagement among firms that adopted a team-managed structure.[2] I wanted to see how engaged the teams were and how involved (or not) the CEO was. Ruston Hughes described Odyssey Engineering Group's management evolution to me:

> The other thing that's helped us grow was the constant evolution of how the company has been managed. As we've grown, that has had to evolve constantly. And I think that Justin and Megan realized when and where to trust people to take the reins or certain aspects of the company and let them have at it. I think that has been critical as well. The way that we needed to run, manage, and operate five years ago is not the same way we needed to do it three years ago; it's not the same as ten years ago or as it is today. So it's constantly evolving.

The BFGs exhibited a relatively broad range of how hands-on the CEOs were. A few CEOs said they weren't very involved in the day-to-day operations, but their leadership team members told me sheepishly that they were. As I dug into the responses, I realized that the CEOs generally got more involved in problem areas or areas they felt were uncovered. Like most founders, CEOs, and entrepreneurs, we all have a bit of a control freak in us, but we need to recognize when to let go and let our teams take over.

I experienced this personally. Eighteen months before I sold my consulting firm to KPMG, I stepped back from the day-to-day business, and we grew even faster! At first, it was a blow to my ego, but then I realized that my leadership was stifling our growth. Fortunately, the team stepped up. It only took me about eight years to figure that out; our BFGs figured it out before I did.

I particularly like how Robert Brill described his involvement with Brill Media. He has a very competent team of executives leading the company. Still, he told me that he regularly changed his relationship with the company based on what he felt it needed at the moment. Some days he might be CFO, and other days he might be the COO or CEO. Once he thought that his functional relationship wasn't needed any longer, he'd move on to a new relationship:

> My job changes every six to twelve months, like the seat right now. I'm the CFO. Not because I want to be a CFO, but because now I know what we need for our business at this moment in time is to be tighter on our invoicing and billing, for example. So I'm not changing my title to the CFO anywhere, but you know that's what I'm doing. I've previously served as the CMO doing marketing and advertising for the business. My relationship with the business is where I loop back around to founder or chairman or some other

> thing that indicates I'm not in the business. That's the ultimate goal.

A team-managed company isn't just a different organizational structure; it's a different way of thinking about work and collaboration. The bootstrapped fast growth of our BFGs highlights that this is the right approach. The culture of innovation, decentralized decision-making, and employee empowerment truly sets these companies apart. More than just a nice option, a team-managed company is a necessity for sustainable growth and scale.

The most successful CEOs in our study figured out how to hire well and then had an effective delegation process with shared outcome-based measurements and clear accountability. I know it was a struggle for many of them to give up control, but just like my company had, their companies flourished and grew faster when they did.

Many shared with me that there was a certain point when they updated their websites and marketing materials to remove them as the founder or CEO entirely or reduced their public visibility. They didn't want customers, prospects, and partners reaching out to them directly anymore, which was a difficult transition in some B2B cases. Coincidentally, it also happened to be the time when they went back to their lenders to remove the personal guarantees they had. Several remarked that that was when they knew they had a scalable organization that was not primarily reliant on them.

Achieving True Scale

Don Wenner started as a top-performing residential real estate agent in the economically challenged Lehigh Valley of Pennsylvania near Allentown. (If you don't know Allentown, check out the song by Bill Joel.) Under Don's leadership, DLP has transformed into an investment giant with more than $5 billion in assets under management, twenty-six hundred investors, and more than eighteen thousand housing units.

They've achieved remarkable growth and scale every year primarily because of the systems and processes they put in place. The internal system that keeps everyone aligned and accountable is called the Elite Execution System, which provides the tools and roadmap to help DLP achieve extraordinary growth. Not only does DLP use this set of tools and processes to scale their own company, but they also license this to their community of investors to help them grow and scale their companies. (Check out Don's best-selling book that details the Elite Execution System model, *Building an Elite Organization: The Blueprint to Scaling a High-Growth, High-Profit Business*.)

DLP invested significant money and human capital to build and deploy this system. Their leadership team admitted that they can spend one to one and one-half hours *per day* in meetings around the Elite Execution System and that their days can be directed toward action items dictated by the Elite Execution System. Some team members acknowledged that an environment like DLP's of complete alignment and strict accountability may not be for everyone, but clearly, it's working for them! This is mainly because Don strives to make DLP the most productive company in the world and the best at scaling. He didn't set a goal of increasing DLPs enterprise value for strictly financial reasons—he did it because he wanted to make an impact. Don's long-term goal (yep, his BHAG) is to increase the wealth and prosperity of ten million people and for DLP to become a Fortune 500 company.

Growing to the point of scale—and only you can determine what that specific point in your growth curve is—offers you options, personally and professionally. As mentioned throughout the book, a few firms were sold during this project, and a few founding CEOs stepped up into chair of the board or founder roles and handed over the reins to full-time CEOs.

Once a company reaches the point of scale where the flywheel is turning on its own, to borrow a Jim Collins concept, it's time to pay special attention to other matters like enterprise value and risk. Doing so will shine a light on various aspects of the business that you may have ignored before, like sales or profit leakage, risk controls, recurring revenue streams, dependence on key employees, or auditable financial records.

My friend and business partner, John Warrilow, author of *Built to Sell*, would argue that the CEO should focus on enterprise value from the beginning and less on the pace of growth (although growth rates are a factor in valuations). Still, very few of our BFGs thought twice about it on their growth journeys. Even when companies were acquired, they were generally opportunistic acquisitions and not a strategic and proactive exit process.

When I asked each CEO how much their company was worth, only three out of fifty had a number, and only one was based on a formal valuation (even though they're not even considering selling). I wasn't surprised to hear they weren't thinking about the value of the company because they were solely focused on growing the business.

One business I spoke with had begun strategically thinking about business worth and risk at a broader company level. RIVA has grown from $1.5 million in revenue to more than $85 million in seven years. As they contemplate what's next, they want to ensure that no secret dragons are hiding around the corner to stunt their growth or put the business at risk. They started having weekly risk meetings and created an Enterprise Risk Dashboard for the company. I mentioned that it sounds awfully corporate and asked if it meant they had hit their stride and relaxed a bit. (I asked this of all the CEOs.) Their COO, Neelu, chuckled and demurred that they have a Day One philosophy and remain healthfully paranoid:

> For the last two years, we've been focused heavily on quality and the idea that we need to be measuring enterprise risk, understanding where the fail points are.

> Being really, really cognizant of that. We have a weekly Enterprise Risk meeting now. I've got a team of folks that sit around the table, and we talk about what could kill us. And it's a great conversation because people don't recognize how many things in their department could destroy the company. Potentially, what kind of risks they have, whether it's PII or whether it's data breach security, whether it's HR, there's a number of different things, so we've done a lot to be able to infuse quality. That led to a lot of automation to secure the ranks, if you will, and make sure that information is tightened up. It's interesting—you implement automation, and you're thinking, okay, things are getting better, better, better, better, better. Then, automation breaks at one point because you get overly reliant on it. For instance, you assume that your cruise control will work, right? I mean, I've got a Tesla. I use it in autonomous mode all the time. But every once in a while, it'll give me a little scare, and I'm like, oh, shit, I should be a little bit more mindful of what I'm doing here.

Most CEOs and business owners believe the best way to improve the value of their company is to make more profit—so they find ways to sell more. And typically selling more means the owner is working harder doing the selling or creating new strategic partnerships. It's natural that customers and key partners want to personally engage with the business owner, which means they are spending more time on the phones, on the road, and face-to-face to increase sales.

With this model, a company can still grow, but the owner's life becomes much more complicated. Customers demand more time and service; employees begin to burn out, and soon it feels like there are not enough hours in the day. Revenue flatlines; health can suffer, and relationships get strained from working too much.

The value of your business comes down to a single equation: What multiple of your profit is an acquirer willing to pay for your company (profit times multiple equals value). Focusing on driving your multiple (the other number in the equation) can help you grow your company's enterprise value and help you achieve greater personal freedom. When you reach this point, you need to change yourself (as I discuss in Part V) and your company. Focusing on improving risk, increasing recurring revenue, doubling down on your differentiated market position, and developing your team will allow you to truly step back from the day-to-day operations and let your leaders flourish and grow.

> Check out our Resources section at www.scaleupfaster.com/resources to download our ebook *The 8 Key Drivers of Company Value*.

PART V

Leadership

I see my mom drop her head into her hands and shake her head with parental admonition: Geez, Pete, did you really need to say that?! I was being given an award for student leader of the year in college, and for my acceptance speech I led with this line: "A great leader is someone who tells you to go to hell . . . and you look forward to the trip." Let's just say in a crowd of almost three hundred people, I only got a few nervous laughs. I've matured a little bit since (although others would disagree), and I have been fascinated by and curious about the idea of leadership since college. I wanted to understand what X factor these founders, CEOs, and their respective leadership teams had that enabled them to grow at the pace they did on a bootstrapped basis.

Chapter 19 tries to answer that question. I asked the founders and CEOs a lot of questions about their backgrounds, whether they had started other companies, what drove them, and how they would describe themselves. I then asked their leadership teams how they would describe these CEOs, what their biggest areas for professional development were, and what made them special.

The spoiler alert is that they're not so different from you and me. So, if you want to achieve the extraordinary level of success that these BFG leaders have, you can.

Chapter 19

LEADING A BFG COMPANY

Strategy in small businesses is like lines in the sand. The tide comes in and wipes it out every day.

—NAVEEN KRISHNAMURTHY, RIVA SOLUTIONS

KEY INSIGHTS

- Align the team with transparency and a set of consistent and meaningful performance indicators.
- Lean into that chip on your shoulder.
- The CEO and leadership team must grow as fast as the company.
- Know when to fire yourself.

How to Align the Team: The North Star Metric

Not everything that counts can be counted,
and not everything that can be counted counts.
—ATTRIBUTED TO ALBERT EINSTEIN

I saw a LinkedIn post listing the KPIs every executive should track. The list had twenty-seven KPIs! There's no way any business leader will track twenty-seven companywide measures without running into issues with metrics that contradict each other, confusion for the team on what to focus on, and metrics that probably don't move the needle in the big scheme of things.

Work hard to pick a North Star Metric (NSM) that everyone can align around and that provides critical input for the company's overall success. The NSM is the key measure that best captures the core value your product delivers to customers. This metric directly ties to the company's growth and long-term success by focusing on sustainable value rather than short-term gains. Unlike vanity metrics that might look impressive on paper but offer little insight into the business's health, the NSM is deeply indicative of a company's future and serves several pivotal roles:

1. Alignment: It aligns all teams and efforts around a singular goal, ensuring everyone is working toward the same objective.
2. Focus: It helps companies focus on what truly matters and avoid the distraction of metrics that don't contribute to the core value proposition.
3. Decision-making: It guides strategic decisions, from product development to marketing strategies, ensuring that all initiatives contribute to enhancing the core value measured by the NSM.
4. Leading indicator: A well-crafted NSM can be a leading indicator of success. It can predict future growth and provide foresight for companies to react and adapt before facing downturns.

The BFGs that had clearly defined and aligned around an NSM (some didn't call it that) saw improved employee retention rates, higher customer LTVs, and faster revenue growth.

JCW's most significant inflection point was when they started measuring performance management using real-time data. They grew faster and hit their stride when they measured the business for the key inputs that drove growth. It wasn't twenty-seven metrics; it was three. Once they did this and shared it with the team, everyone started pulling in one direction, and the company's growth rate soared. But be careful what you measure and how you think about it. As Et Halstead said:

> I would say that what we do have every so often is *Moneyball* moments, as we call them. I imagine you've read *Moneyball* or seen the movie. We're very, very keen on data. And data is really, really dangerous, right? Because you can use it to prove almost anything. So you have to go into data analysis with an open mind.[1]

Developing your NSM or key number(s) is worth the effort. For instance, Acacia (now Mindpath College Health) tracked many internal numbers to determine how they were doing. When they couldn't align all of them perfectly, they settled on a single number to track and influence—not revenue, profit, cash flow, or clinician utilization—but patient show-up rate. This single number affected every other metric. If they achieved above a certain show rate, which they knew was their break-even point, every single percentage above that resulted in increased revenue, profits, and cash flow. I have been coaching a CEO of a similar clinic, and he independently came to the same conclusion. Not only did this number drive all other financial metrics for them, but it was highly operational, as everyone in the company knew how they could positively affect this number.

Finding your NSM will help you communicate precisely what the company is trying to achieve, and like the North Star, it rarely changes over time. And there's only one of them! You will have departmental metrics that each team can influence, but these departmental intermediate measures should directly affect the NSM.

Once you have this figured out, communicate it widely and often! Could you imagine if your favorite sports teams didn't know the score while on the field, court, or pitch? That's precisely what so many business leaders do to their teams, and they wonder why they didn't get the desired results. It's because no one on their team knew how they were doing. When you share the score with your team, it lets them know that you trust them and puts them in a position to help you figure out how to reach the goal. If they know you're twenty points behind, you can work as a team to figure out how to come from behind and win.

How much information should you share?

I'm not a big fan of open-book management. Without deep and consistent education on what the numbers mean, the non-financial types may not truly understand how their day-to-day work translates into affecting the numbers. This approach works for many companies, but you must have the kind of culture where radical transparency is accepted and you invest in educating your team to help them understand how the company's operations affect the financial statements. Kurt Donnell explained to me how he thinks about transparency:

> I'm a big believer in transparency. Be as transparent as you possibly can. This is down to every employee because they will feel more empowered and will trust you as the leader because of it. Since the day I got here, we have done all-hands where we share top-line revenue performance with the entire company weekly and exactly how we're doing against our plan, down to the different business lines, because everybody can make an impact. If needed, let's go find the nickels in the couch

> because they are all over the place, but it will take everybody to find them, and that little 1 percent here and there adds up a lot.[2]

Once you agree on the correct numbers to share with the team and how each person can positively affect that number in their department or role, it's time to put together a companywide platform and cadence for keeping everyone in sync. The frequency of communication is somewhat affected by the velocity of your business. For instance, if you are in the B2B space with twelve-to-eighteen-month sales cycles, a semimonthly review of key drivers of your NSM may be sufficient. (I know a few people will disagree with me on this.) If you are in the B2C space running paid ads every day, you may need to opt for daily or weekly updates. Our BFGs were all over the place in this regard; some companies had daily huddles (very few), many had weekly updates, and the rest had at least monthly updates. The most important thing is to agree on and stick with a cadence.

I mentioned earlier that the team at DLP Capital spends one to one-and-a-half hours every day in meetings getting aligned and focusing on accountability and planning. They review their plans after each specific effort is completed to see how well their plans went. This system developed into their Elite Execution System, which they see as a result of (not the driver of) their success. If that seems too much for you, just remember that they have been on the *Inc.* 5000 for twelve years running and have a solid culture of individual accountability. (You can run, but you can't hide.) Whether or not you hold daily huddles like Verne Harnish and many others recommend is up to you, but there's no such thing as too much communication. Let your teams (and the broader community) know how you are doing!

Here is a more extreme version of this concept, straight from me to you: What if you built failure into the company metrics? Only a few of our BFGs tracked their experiments (A/B testing, etc.) formally, but they all did extensive tests to scale and grow faster. None of them made this a key metric to track. They tested customer segments, product features, message-to-market matches, and other factors. What if you created an intermediate measure of how often you fail each day? How many tests/experiments have you run? With so many things changing in our world and the need to constantly innovate, evolve, and stay at least one step ahead of your competitors, consider incorporating failure as a key measure.

What Skills Do You Need to Be the Leader of a BFG?

I was pleasantly surprised how humble and egoless the founders I spoke to were. Several founders had stepped aside as CEOs and let others take the glory and credit for their company's success. They all refused to accept individual credit for their collective success, which reinforced the idea that their teams were fundamental to how and why they had accomplished so much.

When I asked the CEOs to describe themselves, the words they used most often were driven, authentic, thoughtful, useful, tenacious, motivated, determined, resourceful, confident, and innovative. I then asked their teams to describe the founder or CEO, and most of the same adjectives were used. At least I know the founders and CEOs were self-aware.

I then asked each of the founders or CEOs what single trait a person needed to pull off the kind of bootstrapped growth they had experienced. The traits they mentioned included self-motivation, curiosity, passion, and fearlessness, conviction, and resilience. But the skill mentioned most frequently was grit. (Angela Duckworth would be pleased to hear this.) Even though this is a book about success, virtually all these companies stumbled enough times that the leaders had to pick themselves up and keep going, so the level of grittiness was evident. Some of the BFGs made wholesale shifts in strategy, most hired (and fired) the wrong people, many nearly ran out of cash, and all faced significant hurdles at each phase of their growth. Christina Stembel exemplifies grit:

> You know, I'm not the smartest. I don't have the most experience or the best education. I don't have any of the things. But it's like Will Smith said, the one thing is he'll die on the treadmill. I'll die on the treadmill. I'll get back up every single time.[3]

Every founder and CEO felt like they hadn't fully hit their stride, and although many of them have hundreds of millions of dollars of revenue and very healthy bottom lines and bank accounts, they still felt like failure could be just around the corner. They truly lived Andy Grove's (the cofounder of Intel) philosophy: only the paranoid survive. Find your grit belt, strap it on tight, and know your journey of bootstrapped high growth will be filled with many moments when you live to fight another day.

If you want to grow your company faster and with sustainable scale, you'll have to set aside your ego, forget that your way is the only way, be okay with giving up control, and put on an extra-large size of your trust pants.

Lean into That Chip on Your Shoulder

Christina grew up in a midwestern town with parents who believed in the old ways of thinking—boys worked, got an education, and provided for the family. Girls? They were supposed to look cute, get married, have kids, and settle down. So, after discovering that her parents had hired a financial planner to help them pay for her younger brother's college but not hers, this set her on a path to prove to her parents that she would make her own success, despite being a girl. Christina shared her story with me:

> I actually think my brother and I are a really good social science experiment, because we were raised in the same house: my sister, my brother, and me. . . . My sister and I are almost identical in age; we're nine months, seven days apart. . . . So my parents had the same amount of resources and means available at that time. And then my brother is four years younger, and a boy, and in a gender-role environment, that's where you put all of your eggs—in that basket of the boy. They started saving for college for him, and my sister and I were supposed to get married and have kids, and things like that. I have, and will, make my own success. I will go live in a car if I have to. I will literally drink tea and eat ramen every day, I will pay myself $60,000 a year and live in a one-bedroom apartment as a CEO of a company for a decade.

Kyle Mitnick grew up in an upper-middle-class home in Southern California. His dad was a doctor who assumed (wrongly) that his son would become a doctor too. When he was in high school, Kyle loved to surf, and nothing else. But between catching waves, he started seeing the internet craze and thought, "Wow, this is so lucrative!" Like many aspiring entrepreneurs, he started small companies, like an online clothing company in high school. It was a successful venture for a high school kid, but despite this, he felt that his dad would never give him the time of day. After a while, when they both realized that he wasn't going to fulfill his dad's dream of having his son become a doctor, that was it; he knew he was never going to get his dad's attention or the validation he was seeking. So, as perverse as it sounds, success in his business is partly because he sought his dad's attention and respect. Kyle shared his story with me:

> I grew up in a family that has a long lineage of doctors or lawyers. You were either one of the two; that was just the way that it was, if you wanted to be respected. It was a fairly cerebral academic family. I never quite fit into that early on. . . . I was definitely smart, but I didn't want to put the time in like people around me. . . . I was starting to see this whole internet craze and I'm like, what is this? This is way more lucrative. I could buy way more surfboards doing this than being a doctor. . . . I started these small companies in high school, these clothing companies, and my dad was just like, "What are you doing? That's a waste of time." And I could never get his attention. . . . He would never give me the time of day. . . . So this entire road that I've been on is . . . to get his attention, and I still don't have it today. . . . So I think that's what the chip on my shoulder is—I'll show you. Start the company in 2012, get ten employees, look at that. That's more employees than your practice had, Dad. Goes to fifty, we start getting awards, look at this, Dad. . . . I started making investments and personal financial decisions that are visible to people in my family. Look at that, Dad. And so it's been, and it remains today. Like, this is the right choice. Why don't you admit it?[4]

Naveen worked for his father-in-law, a minority investor in the business. It's tough working with family, but after Naveen decided to strike out on his own to start RIVA, the family turned against him because they were all on the payroll, and sales declined when he left. The family blessed his departure, but it ultimately led to his divorce, and the business he left suffered. The company wound up failing, and he lost almost everything he'd built. Naveen's chip became his way to say, hey, can I do better than them. After the divorce and losing everything, being single and without a company to lead, he wanted to prove to his ex and her family that he could build everything back up and then some—which he did, and much faster than he thought he'd be able to.[5]

David Freedman started a swimsuit calendar company during his senior year in college. The business was incredibly successful and eventually expanded to multiple colleges. Because he was known as the "swimsuit calendar guy," he wasn't taken seriously as a real businessperson. It didn't help that he looked young. So when he started his next venture, Freestar, he had an axe to grind. He *was* a serious businessperson with serious ideas and was intent on proving to everyone that his previous business and age didn't define him—he would be a successful entrepreneur. David shared his story with me:

> I think it's a little bit of maturity with age. . . . With my first company, we sold advertising in a half a million calendars distributed across twenty-one schools, and I literally just had two interns and one employee. Because of the nature of my business, everyone had their opinion of me without knowing me. "Oh, he's some scummy guy taking advantage of girls," or "This is a BS company," or whatever. People didn't understand the actual business behind it, and I think it created a huge chip on my shoulder of, I'm going to go prove everyone wrong. It was truly a me-against-the-world mentality and just being way too stubborn to fail. I took it as a personal challenge to succeed, and I think I did.[6]

Megan Crutcher started Odyssey Engineering Group because she was working sixty to seventy hours a week while she was six months pregnant with her second child. She asked for relief from the insane hours for more than two years, and she never got it. She was pissed. She cofounded Odyssey Engineering Group with Justin Ring who, at his previous company, had been one of the youngest partners up for a leadership position to run one of their business units. He lost out to someone several years older and figured that it could be a decade before he got another shot. Because he felt that he'd lost because of seniority and not performance, he quit and cofounded the company with Megan to prove to the owners of his former company that they had picked the wrong guy.[7]

What do all these stories have in common? These founders and CEOs all had a chip on their shoulders.

They had to prove something to someone—parents, an ex-spouse, themselves. They all consciously or unconsciously leaned into their chips as their driving motivation to build, grow, and scale their companies. They were never settled with a lifestyle business or a small, irrelevant one. They wanted to make a very visible splash and a very visible impact. Christina Stembel explained this eloquently:

> I think the highest performers, at least the highest performers on my team, all have chips on their shoulders. They were told they're not good enough. They're not smart enough. I know exactly what it is. I see it because that's what drives them. Every high performer I've ever worked with has a chip. So my chip is that nobody believed in me. I wasn't given the opportunity that I wanted to have as a female. So that's my chip, I'm not good enough. Nobody values me, so I'm going to show them. That's really what it is. Let me show them.

None of these CEOs are exceptional with respect to their background, experience, education, or leg up. They were all exceptional at growing, learning, falling, getting up, and asking for help. They didn't have grand visions to conquer the world; they just wanted to create a substantial business in a space that was important to them.

They used their chips to drive them forward. Indeed, they all achieved extraordinary things in their businesses and lives and have received ample validation from many stakeholders—but not the ones that mattered most to them. They were also open to personal development and growth.

RIVA Solutions even looks for employees with an ambitious chip on their shoulders because they know it provides the internal motivation to try harder to accomplish their goals. If you are mad at the world about something and are leading an organization, use it for good by leaning into it and letting it drive you (but without driving your team away).

When to Fire Yourself

If you're truly going to commit to building a great company, a strong leadership team, and getting the right people in the right seats, you must prepare for change on your leadership team.
—**GINO WICKMAN, *Traction***

In 2007, Reid Hoffman, the founder of LinkedIn, stepped down as the CEO. At the time, LinkedIn had only nine million members. They now have one billion.

Why did he step down so early in LinkedIn's growth trajectory? Because he knew that he was not the right person to run a company of that size at the time. Although he became LinkedIn CEO for a short period one more time, he knew he had made the right decision. He understood that you need the right leader at the right time.

Christina Stembel learned this the hard way. Son Pham told me what Christina said about how she decided to invest in hiring a leadership team:

> She tells people that before she hired a leadership team, she always thought she couldn't afford one—until those big mistakes happened. And when those big mistakes mounted to millions and millions of dollars, she realized that it was actually more costly not to have one. That's where she had an epiphany and started building a leadership team around her.[8]

I'm not suggesting that you need to step down as the founder or CEO, but we all have skills and abilities that may or may not be appropriate for your company's growth stage. At least four founders or CEOs passed the reins to more professional managers because they knew in their hearts that they were entrepreneurs, not managers. The same goes for leaders on your team. Zack Onisko told me what finally allowed him to let go a little:

> In those early days, I was the bottleneck for all things. So all decisions had to roll through me. And you know, of course, once you start to scale up the team that's not sustainable. Once we started to build the leadership team and bring in great managers, then I could kind of let go of the reins and let them run their teams.[9]

When I asked the CEOs what was most challenging about being a CEO, almost universally the answer was having to move people out of the company who had contributed to the company's early growth. I heard several stories about nasty battles with cofounders who had to be bought out, fired, or both. David Freedman shared with me just how difficult these decisions can be—but also how beneficial they can be for all parties in the long run:

> Also having a really, really tough look in the mirror of making the tough decisions on people you just adore. You may love that they have helped you get to a certain point, but they're just not the right person to get you to that next level. That's one of the toughest personal challenges because I genuinely care about the people on the team. You know how much some of them truly put in from an effort standpoint. But at a certain point, though, it's forcing a square peg into a round hole. While it sucked in the moment, it's also realizing that when something doesn't fit, it's equally as uncomfortable for them. They might not be speaking up so once you call it, set them free. Most of the time, they're really grateful even though they don't feel like that in the beginning.

Not every company faced this, but most of the larger ones did have to make substantial leadership changes as they scaled. To scale faster, it is critical to look at your leadership team and yourself in the mirror to determine whether you have the right people on board to make it to the next level of growth and scale.

And if not, act accordingly.

Of course, it doesn't always mean you have to terminate them. Still, you do need to have the difficult conversation with them (and again, perhaps have a conversation with yourself) and say that there is someone else who can do a better job of leading the company to the next stage of growth but there is still a place in the organization for them where you can take advantage of their skills and allow them to grow. Several BFG CEOs lamented that they took too long to make these decisions, and their growth suffered as a result. It's natural to remain loyal to those who helped you get where you are, but as Marshall Goldsmith famously said in his book, what brought you here won't get you there. Carlos Chilin, with Advertise Purple, talked about how well Kyle Mitnick managed this issue:

> I think Kyle has done well in identifying in himself what he does well, which is that kind of entrepreneurial idea generation, ideation, proliferation of growth, et cetera. And I'm the opposite of that. For example, when I came into my previous company, it was a company that had existed for fifteen years. I know my strengths, and my strengths aren't necessarily on the entrepreneurial side, but I can come into a business that has something going and optimize it and find efficiencies in the operations, standardize and stabilize it—mature it to a good level. I think if he didn't have that self-awareness, if he didn't understand himself, he might have brought in someone else who was just as entrepreneurial as he was and maybe missed some of the details that are crucial in building that kind of stable infrastructure that are benefiting us today.[10]

Chapter 20

FINAL THOUGHTS

Every leader who gave me so much of their time is truly wealthy. I was inspired not only by the rates of growth they achieved and all their corporate accomplishments but also by their passion, vision, caring, and desire to make themselves, their companies, their teams, and their communities better—including you, my dear reader.

Some of the companies were overtly mission-focused, like DLP Capital, but they all had a strong desire to make a positive impact in the world. Although I've known quite a few venture-backed companies and their leaders, they somehow don't seem to have the same level of authenticity as our BFGs. I don't know whether it's a function of the fact that the BFGs started with nothing and had to scrape and scratch for every ounce of growth and that journey is indelible in their minds, but connecting with them felt refreshing and honest.

Although very few of our BFGs will be multibillion-dollar companies, in my humble opinion, they will make a much bigger impact than their corporate brethren because they don't do it for the money, the exit potential, or the fame. They grow faster because by doing so, they can make a bigger impact in the world.

I never sensed any fakeness or lip service in the leaders I spent time with. They were and are just a bunch of extraordinarily ordinary folks making life better for themselves and all of us.

Here's to growing and scaling faster so you can make a bigger impact too!

NOTES

PREAMBLE

1. Carolyn Dewar, Scott Keller, and Vikram Malhotra, "Author Talks: What Separates the Best CEOs from the Rest?," interview by Raju Narisetti, McKinsey and Company, December 15, 2021, https://www.mckinsey.com/featured-insights/mckinsey-on-books/author-talks-what-separates-the-best-ceos-from-the-rest.

INTRODUCTION

1. Kyle Mitnick, Zoom interview by the author, January 31, 2023. All other quotations from Kyle Mitnick in this chapter come from this interview.
2. Rebecca Szkutak, "Early-Stage SaaS Startups Grow the Same with or without VC Dollars," *TechCrunch*, July 20, 2023, https://techcrunch.com/2023/07/20/early-stage-saas-startups-vc-bootstrap/.
3. Szkutak, "Early-Stage SaaS Startups."
4. David George, "The Year to Be Great," Andreessen Horowitz, February 29, 2024, https://a16z.com/the-year-to-be-great.
5. Scott Andrew, Zoom interview by the author, November 7, 2022.
6. *Inc.* 5000 is a copyright of Mansueto Ventures.
7. All currency values in this book are in U.S. dollars.
8. Daniel Evans, Zoom interview by the author, January 13, 2023.
9. KorbyQuan Reed, Zoom interview by the author, February 1, 2023.

10. Alex Love, Zoom interview by the author, September 6, 2023.
11. Lawrence Scotland, Zoom interview by the author, November 17, 2022. All other quotations from Lawrence Scotland come from this interview.
12. Kat Taylor Simonyi, Zoom interview by the author, November 3, 2022.
13. Darren Conrad, Zoom interview by the author, February 22, 2023.
14. Russell Brunson, interview by the author, April 9, 2023.
15. Neil Patel, Zoom interview by the author, October 30, 2023.

CHAPTER 1

1. Kyle Mitnick, Zoom interview by the author, January 31, 2023.
2. Don Wenner, Zoom interview by the author, August 26, 2022. All other quotations from Don Wenner in Part I come from this interview.
3. Megan Crutcher and Justin Ring, Zoom interview by the author, November 28, 2022.
4. Aasha Anam, Zoom interview by the author, August 14, 2023. All other quotations from Aasha Anam in Part I come from this interview.
5. Robert Brill, Zoom interview by the author, April 28, 2023.
6. Nina McQueen, "Workplace Culture Trends: The Key to Hiring (and Keeping) Top Talent in 2018," *LinkedIn Official Blog*, June 26, 2018, https://www.linkedin.com/blog/member/career/workplace-culture-trends-the-key-to-hiring-and-keeping-top-talent.
7. Lindsey Whalen Draska, Zoom interview by the author, October 21, 2022. All other quotations from Lindsey Whalen Draska in Part I come from this interview.
8. Jonathan Moisan, Zoom interview by the author, May 8, 2023. All other quotations from Jonathan Moisan in Part I come from this interview.
9. Capital Brand Group, "Careers," accessed March 26, 2024, https://capitalbrandgroup.com/careers/.
10. PRX Performance, "About Us," accessed March 26, 2024, https://prxperformance.com/pages/about-us-2021.
11. Pendo, "About," accessed March 2, 2024, https://www.pendo.io/about/.
12. ShipBob, "Careers," accessed March 26, 2024, https://www.shipbob.com/careers/.
13. Dribbble, "Careers," accessed March 26, 2024, https://dribbble.com/careers.
14. GenTech Associates, "Careers," accessed March 26, 2024, https://gentechassociates.com/careers/.

15. Bobby Frazitta, Zoom interview by the author, October 6, 2023. All other quotations from Bobby Frazitta in Part I come from this interview.
16. TestGorilla, "The State of Skills-Based Hiring, 2023," accessed March 19, 2024, https://assets.ctfassets.net/vztl6s0hp3ro/5B8Km5VxEDgdx0VhLQTjdX/c27d9e5af3209bf6580e0b52813a7d23/TestGorilla-The-state-of-skills-based-hiring-report-2023.pdf.
17. TestGorilla, "The State of Skills-Based Hiring."
18. TestGorilla, "The State of Skills-Based Hiring 2023," 16.
19. Chloe Oddleifson, Zoom interview by the author, October 20, 2022. All other quotations from Chloe Oddleifson in Part I come from this interview.

CHAPTER 2

1. Laszlo Bock, *Work Rules! Insights from Inside Google That Will Transform How You Live and Lead* (New York: Twelve, 2015).
2. Ellen Hughes, Zoom interview by the author, January 30, 2023. All other quotations from Ellen Hughes in Part I come from this interview.
3. Christy Rosensteel, Zoom interview by the author, June 20, 2023. All other quotations from Christy Rosensteel in Part I come from this interview.

CHAPTER 3

1. Kate Turner, Zoom interview by the author, July 17, 2023. All other quotations from Kate Turner in Part I come from this interview.
2. David Novak, "Here's the No. 1 Reason Why Employees Quit Their Jobs," *NBC News*, June 21, 2019, https://www.nbcnews.com/better/lifestyle/here-s-no-1-reason-why-employees-quit-their-jobs-ncna1020031.
3. Kurt Donnell, Zoom interview by the author, June 30, 2022.
4. Kyle Mitnick, Zoom interview by the author, February 3, 2023.
5. Jim Harter and Amy Adkins, "Employees Want a Lot More from Their Managers," Gallup, April 8, 2015, https://www.gallup.com/workplace/236570/employees-lot-managers.aspx.
6. Jim Clifton, "It's the Manager," Gallup, May 7, 2019, https://www.gallup.com/workplace/251642/manager.aspx.

CHAPTER 4

1. Lori Goler, Janelle Gale, Brynn Harrington, and Adam Grant, "Why People Really Quit Their Jobs," *Harvard Business Review*, January 11, 2018, https://hbr.org/2018/01/why-people-really-quit-their-jobs.

PART II

1. Brian Dean, "Here's What We Learned about Organic Click Through Rate," Backlinko, May 28, 2023, https://backlinko.com/google-ctr-stats.

CHAPTER 6

1. Wesley Germain, "How to Budget for and Build a Marketing Organization Fit for Growth," LLR Partners, 2023, https://www.llrpartners.com/growth-bit/how-to-budget-build-a-marketing-organization-for-growth/.
2. Kyle Mitnick, Zoom interview by the author, July 26, 2023. All other quotations from Kyle Mitnick in this chapter come from this interview.
3. Alex Hormozi, *$100M Leads: How to Get Strangers to Want to Buy Your Stuff* (Austin, TX: Acquisition.com, 2023), 424.
4. Michael Sacca, Zoom interview by the author, October 27, 2022.
5. Russell Brunson, interview by the author, April 9, 2023.
6. Kat Taylor Simonyi, Zoom interview by the author, November 3, 2022. All other quotations from Kat Taylor in this chapter come from this interview.
7. Christina Stembel, Zoom interview by the author, December 16, 2022. All other quotations from Christina Stembel in this chapter come from this interview.
8. Don Wenner, Zoom interview by the author, August 26, 2022. All other quotations from Don Wenner in Part II come from this interview.

CHAPTER 7

1. Jerry Williams, Zoom interview by the author, February 14, 2023.
2. Todd Caponi, *The Transparency Sale: How Unexpected Honesty and Understanding the Buying Brain Can Transform Your Results* (Washington, DC: Ideapress, 2018).
3. Fred Reichheld with Rob Markey, *The Ultimate Question 2.0: How Net Promoter Companies Thrive in a Customer-Driven World*, rev. and expanded ed. (Boston: Harvard Business Review Press, 2011).

4. Kurt Donnell, Zoom interview by the author, June 30, 2022.
5. David Freedman, Zoom interview by the author, September 7, 2023.

CHAPTER 8

1. John Newton, Zoom interview by the author, January 11, 2023.
2. Linda Monsour, Zoom interview by the author, June 14, 2023.
3. Nathan Latka, "How ClickFunnels Built a $160m Revenue Empire, $5 Billing+ Exit in 2023?," *LATKA—B2B SaaS Blog*, January 16, 2023, https://blog.getlatka.com/clickfunnels-what-is-revenue/.

CHAPTER 9

1. Christina Fiasconaro, Zoom interview by the author, July 25, 2023.
2. Sufian Munir, Zoom interview by the author, August 9, 2023.

PART III

1. Neelu Modali, Zoom interview by the author, October 31, 2023.

CHAPTER 10

1. Verne Harnish, *Scaling Up: How a Few Companies Make It . . . and Why the Rest Don't* (Kindle edition, 2022), 137.
2. Kurt Donnell, Zoom interview by the author, June 30, 2022. All other quotations from Kurt Donnell in Part III come from this interview.
3. Brandon Green, Zoom interview by the author, October 31, 2022. All other quotations from Brandon Green in Part III come from this interview.
4. Scott Andrew, Zoom interview by the author, July 24, 2023. All other quotations from Scott Andrew in this chapter come from this interview.
5. Simon Elsbury, Zoom interview by the author, July 31, 2023. All other quotations from Simon Elsbury in Part III come from this interview.

CHAPTER 11

1. Christina Stembel, Zoom interview by the author, December 16, 2022. All other quotations from Christina Stembel in this chapter come from this interview.
2. Son Pham, Zoom interview by the author, October 26, 2022. All other quotations from Son Pham in this chapter come from this interview.
3. Katya Wachtel, "Warren Buffett: There's Only One Thing That Matters to Me When I'm Investing in a Company," *Business Insider*, February 18, 2011, https://www.businessinsider.com/warren-buffett-pricing-power-beats-good-management-berkshire-hathaway-2011-2.

CHAPTER 14

1. Michael Boyles, "What Is Business Strategy and Why Is It Important?," *Harvard Business Review*, October 20, 2022, https://online.hbs.edu/blog/post/what-is-business-strategy.
2. David Freedman, Zoom interview by the author, September 7, 2023.
3. Don Wenner, Zoom interview by the author, August 26, 2022. All other information on Don Wenner in Part IV comes from this interview.
4. Michael Sacca, Zoom interview by the author, October 27, 2022. All other quotations from Michael Sacca in Part IV come from this interview.
5. Kurt Donnell, Zoom interview by the author, May 30, 2023. All other quotations from Kurt Donnell in Part IV come from this interview.
6. Scott Andrew, Zoom interview by the author, November 7, 2022. All other quotations from Scott Andrew in this chapter come from this interview.
7. Zack Onisko, Zoom interview by the author, September 23, 2022.
8. Et Halstead, Zoom interview by the author, January 5, 2023. All other quotations from Et Halstead in Part IV come from this interview.
9. Christina Stembel, Zoom interview by the author, December 16, 2022. All other quotations from Christina Stembel in this chapter come from this interview.
10. Jim Collins and Morten T. Hansen, *Great by Choice: Uncertainty, Chaos, and Luck—Why Some Thrive Despite Them All* (New York: Harper Business, 2011).
11. Jamie Woods, Zoom interview by the author, October 17, 2022.
12. Jason Zweig, "Charlie Munger's Life Was about Way More Than Money," *Wall Street Journal*, November 29, 2023, https://www.wsj.com/finance/investing/charlie-munger-life-money-ae3853ad.
13. Naveen Krishnamurthy, Zoom interview by the author, December 12, 2022.
14. Kyle Mitnick, Zoom interview by the author, March 3, 2023.

15. Carlos Chilin, Zoom interview by the author, April 26, 2023.
16. Ruston Hughes, Zoom interview by the author, February 7, 2023. All other quotations from Ruston Hughes in Part IV come from this interview.
17. Ashlee Vance, *Elon Musk: Tesla, SpaceX, and the Quest for a Fantastic Future* (New York: HarperCollins, 2017).
18. Kenneth O. Stanley and Joel Lehman, *Why Greatness Cannot Be Planned: The Myth of the Objective* (Cham, Germany: Springer, 2015).

CHAPTER 15

1. Mark Hodges, Zoom interview by the author, January 27, 2023. All other quotations and information from Mark Hodges in Part IV come from this interview.
2. Linda Monsour, Zoom interview by the author, June 14, 2023.
3. Zarrar Kahn, Zoom interview by the author, November 1, 2023.

CHAPTER 16

1. Neelu Modali, Zoom interview by the author, October 31, 2023. All other quotations from Neelu Modali in Part IV come from this interview.
2. Michael Chavira, Zoom interview by the author, August 15, 2022.
3. Robert Brill, Zoom interview by the author, April 28, 2023. All other quotations from Robert Brill in Part IV come from this interview.
4. Salim Ismail, Peter H. Diamandis, and Michael S. Malone, *Exponential Organizations 2.0: The New Playbook for 10× Growth and Impact* (Powell, OH: Ethos Collective, 2023).

CHAPTER 17

1. Robbyn Jackson, Zoom interview by the author, November 7, 2022.
2. Bob Peterson, Zoom interview by the author, September 21, 2022.
3. Kevin Sneader and Shubham Singhal, "The Next Normal Arrives: Trends That Will Define 2021—and Beyond," McKinsey and Company, January 4, 2021, https://www.mckinsey.com/featured-insights/leadership/the-next-normal-arrives-trends-that-will-define-2021-and-beyond.
4. EOS is a registered trademark of EOS Worldwide.

CHAPTER 18

1. Jeffrey P. Bezos, letter to Amazon shareholders, 1997, https://media.corporate-ir.net/media_files/irol/97/97664/reports/Shareholderletter97.pdf.
2. Gary Hamel, "First, Let's Fire All the Managers," *Harvard Business Review*, December 2011, https://hbr.org/2011/12/first-lets-fire-all-the-managers.

CHAPTER 19

1. Et Halstead, Zoom interview by the author, January 5, 2023.
2. Kurt Donnell, Zoom interview by the author, May 30, 2023.
3. Christina Stembel, Zoom interview by the author, December 16, 2022. All other quotations from Christina Stembel in this chapter come from this interview.
4. Kyle Mitnick, Zoom interview by the author, March 3, 2023.
5. Naveen Krishnamurthy, Zoom interview by the author, December 12, 2022. All other quotations from Naveen Krishnamurthy in this chapter come from this interview.
6. David Freedman, Zoom interview by the author, September 7, 2023. All other quotations from David Freedman in this chapter come from this interview.
7. Megan Crutcher and Justin Ring, Zoom interview by the author, November 28, 2022.
8. Son Pham, Zoom interview by the author, October 26, 2022.
9. Zack Onisko, Zoom interview by the author, September 23, 2022.
10. Carlos Chilin, Zoom interview by the author, April 26, 2023.

ADDITIONAL READING

Andrew, Carlton Scott. *The Rugged Entrepreneur: What Every Disruptive Business Leader Should Know.* Nashville, TN: Forefront Books, 2020.

Collins, Jim. *Good to Great: Why Some Companies Make the Leap . . . and Others Don't.* New York: Harper Business, 2001.

Collins, Jim, and Bill Lazier. *Beyond Entrepreneurship 2.0: Turning Your Business into an Enduring Great Company.* New York: Portfolio/Penguin, 2020.

Collins, Jim, and Morten T. Hansen. *Great by Choice: Uncertainty, Chaos, and Luck—Why Some Thrive Despite Them All.* New York: Harper Business, 2011.

Harnish, Verne. *Scaling Up: How a Few Companies Make It . . . and Why the Rest Don't.* Ashburn, VA: Gazelles, 2014.

Marcus Aurelius. *Meditations.* Translated by Gregory Hays. New York: Modern Library, 2003.

Warrilow, John. *The Automatic Customer: Creating a Subscription Business in Any Industry.* New York: Penguin, 2015.

Warrilow, John. *Built to Sell: Creating a Business That Can Thrive without You.* New York: Penguin, 2010.

Wenner, Don. *Building an Elite Organization: The Blueprint to Scaling a High-Growth, High-Profit Business.* Austin, TX: Lioncrest, 2023.

Wickman, Gino. *Traction: Get a Grip on Your Business.* Dallas, TX: BenBella Books, 2012.

Wickman, Gino, and Rob Dube. *Shine: 10 Disciplines for Maximizing Your Energy, Impact, and Inner Peace.* Dallas, TX: BenBella Books, 2024.

ABOUT THE AUTHOR

PETE MARTIN has worked in sales, operations, and executive management for more than twenty-five years, beginning in sales at IBM, then working in executive management at SAP, and then building six of his own companies. He has personally sold more than $1 billion in software, services, and technology to global companies, as well as small and medium-sized businesses. Pete started, scaled, and sold four previous companies (car leasing, systems integration consulting, business process outsourcing, and software distribution) and sold his last firm to global auditing giant KPMG for twelve times EBITDA.

Pete has personally advised hundreds of C-level executives and business owners across twenty-six industries on how to grow their companies faster, enhance their business operations, improve their financial performance, and exit richer.

Pete currently lives in Cleveland, Ohio, and enjoys drumming in a classic rock band.